Embracing

By Christina King

Healing Our Wounds & Reclaiming Our Greatness through Theology of The Body

ISBN 978-1-304-94761-1
90000

9 781304 947611

See all of our books at: www.EmbracingYourGreatness.org

Christina King
Daughter of Our Lady of Guadalupe and Christ The King

Special Thanks to:

My mother, for baptizing me and giving me my faith. My Omi and opi for showing me that a lifetime of marriage can bring out the best in the other. The Kroll family, especially Mrs. Kroll for helping me believe that has called me into being "forever" with God is what I have been made for. The priest that heard my first confession, for giving me courage to tell. My Father for coming to get me and Sue for loving me as her own. The Krause family, for helping me choose life and giving me a book on Natural Family Planning. The Brostrum family and Pat that helped me go to college. The Theology of the Body Institute for providing a place to learn Theology of The Body, which transformed my head and my heart. Dr. Bob Schuchts for sharing his beautiful gifts of healing through the John Paul II Healing Center. Neal Lozano for his work in Deliverance Ministry. Lynn, Fr. Bryce, Vicky, Angie and Kristin for proving to me that I am a gift worth sharing and that I can trust again. My children, for teaching me so much about love. To my husband from whose love and support gave me the courage and strength to go into the most ugly of wounds, you are my precious knight in shining armor. Jessica for edits, Catholic Foundation for funds. Finally, I thank God the Father for wanting me so much that He Chose me out of all of the potential people that He could have created. For Christ my bridegroom, thank you for your tender mercy and the gentle way you take things slow. You never kick in my doors. I thank Mary for her example and her intercession in all of this as well as her spouse the Holy Spirit in which I have become a new creation.

Long Live Christ Our King and Our Lady of Guadalupe

Fr. Peter Stryker CPM Rector of The Shrine of Our Lady of Good Help in Champion, Wisconsin

"Is there anyone who does not need some form of healing in their life? In this fascinating book, Christina opens with a wonderful Gospel promise: That Christ Jesus came into this world to set captives free! And she concludes with a marvelous scriptural reality: The Bible begins and ends with a wedding, and we ourselves are made for a spousal relationship with the Lord of Life who loves each one of us! Christina takes us on a very personal journey, yet ultimately she tells her story so that we could never hesitate to ask, seek, and knock for healing and renewal which belongs to each of us as God's Children."

Fr. Peter Stryker CPM

Father's of Mercy

Cathy, Abuse Survivor

"I wanted to let you know I couldn't put your book down. I have been opened up by your book to new healing that I never knew existed. Now I fully understand the lies that I believed created a lack of intimacy and a desire to control everything because of the sexual, physical, and emotional abuse I experienced as a child. I am looking at my husband and children in a whole new light. Thank you from the bottom of my heart..."

Cathy

Contents

INTRODUCTION

"The Spirit of the Sovereign LORD is on me, because the LORD has anointed me to proclaim good news to the poor. He has sent me to bind up the brokenhearted, to proclaim freedom for the captives and release from darkness for the prisoners" Isaiah 61:1

Christ comes to set the captives free! This is my good news and I wish to proclaim it to those who are brokenhearted so that they too can know that there is freedom and release from the darkness! God does not desire for you to be a prisoner, that is a lie from the pit of hell. I have speaking across the continent for the past 15 years, and over and over again I encounter people who need to find freedom through healing.

The reason I have decided to write this book is because of the freedom I have found on that journey. I experienced physical, sexual, emotionally and psychological abuse. My first memory is of me at age three being sexually abused. For years I struggled to "feel" normal. I wondered why I had such a hard time with affection, trusting people or making and keeping friends. I had begun to believe that I would never be free from the painful memories and the anxiety of just trying to get through a day. Then I encountered Healing Ministry. I have received more healing in the last several years by this method than all of the 30 years of counseling combined. I have now dedicated my life to bringing Christ's healing love to others through Healing Ministry.

I cannot contain my joy for myself, I must share it because I see so many people in my travels that are broken, hurting, alone, lost and suffering under the weight of their own weaknesses and I desire to be someone who can help them carry the weight of their cross. In fact, once we gain freedom from our wounds, they become transformed and begin to radiate Christ to all those around us. Let me share my own journey with you and say a simple prayer of agreement now, "Come Holy Spirit, Come" so that perhaps you too will be made new.

If you or someone you know feels they are nailed to their cross instead of carrying it, then this book may be an answer to prayer. I have endured many different kinds of abuse, and I have gone on to woundothers in the very way in which I am wounded. It is an irony that is not lost on me. However, once I recognized this pattern, I was able to discover the root wounds buried and hidden deep within me. What I have learned is that when I meet people that create a distress in me, it is usually a neon sign, pointing me to an area that within me that needs further healing.

My hope is that my journey to embrace my God-given greatness will not only inspire you but will give you courage. I pray it gives you courage to press into some of the dark places that many of you have not had the courage to go into or perhaps have not had the vulnerability to look at. I know this is a scary thing to ask, but let me be a witness to the reality that God does not disappoint, He does not abandon, He does not force himself on you nor does He take any pleasure in your suffering. In fact, He suffers it. The only way to begin this journey is with vulnerability.

We must be willing to trade in our hearts of stone for a heart of flesh and blood. We must be willing to trust in ways we may never have dared to trust. Do not hold back. Expect Him to create miracles! Ask for a double portion of grace! AllHe wants is you. He wants you to be His and His alone. He loves you and you are His. He wants you to reject the counterfeit bridegroom and to accept His marriage proposal instead. He desires union and communion with your heart, for you to know Him in an intimate and experiential way. How do you begin this journey? It is in being willing to be vulnerable.

It is in being vulnerable that we are able to open ourselves to the Bridegroom. Jesus is the Bridegroom and knows all of the secrets of our story. He desires to make us whole and it is only through His grace that we can be transformed. I am here to say it is not only possible, but also what you might believe to be your greatest flaw or your most ugly secret may just be the birthplace of your greatness.

Come and put your fingers into my wounds so that you too will believe. Open your hearts and minds to not only believe but to receive your own healing because today is the day of freedom!

My Wounded Heart

"Healing is an essential dimension of the apostolic mission and of Christianity. When understood at a sufficiently deep level this expresses the entire content of redemption"

Pope Benedict XVI

From the very beginning of the Bible, 'sin' is defined as *separation from God*. It is also spoken of as a transgression, which means to violate the law. Since the law is meant to protect us, we see that sin is not only a violation against God but also against ourselves and of all creation. When we sin we separate ourselves from God, transgress against His will, against one another, and against all of creation. This is the condition we live in due to original sin.

The word 'sin' can also be understood as *missing the mark*. In archery, 'sin' is a term used when an archer aimed but fell short of the target's center. Many of us aim to please God yet we all fall short of the glory of God.

With these biblical definitions, we can agree that we are all sinners. All of us live in that place of struggle in which we miss the mark, transgress upon the will of God and in doing so violate one another and ourselves.

All of us are sinners and the effects of sin are wounds. Sin wounds every time, not just us, but everyone around us. That being the case, it's very clear that living in this world is impossible without being wounded. Sin is like cancer in that if it's ignored it will grow in our bodies. As Christians we are called to be the body of Christ. We are to make Christ visible in and through our lives. We are to be living signs; our families are to be an icon of the Trinitarian love of God revealing truth, life and love to the world. When we sin, the effects of our sin spreads out into our lives thus marring our ability to reveal Christ to the world.

Sin spreads is all around us in our social relationships. When we sin, we diminish Christ's glory; not that Christ's glory can be diminished, but certainly our ability to be an icon that reveals His Glory can be diminished. How can someone see Christ in us when our sin is the first thing someone sees?

Scripture tells us in Genesis, Exodus and Deuteronomy that sin also has an effect for generations. Some scriptures say ten generations. Many of us are not only dealing with our own sinfulness but with sin that has had it's effects in our families down through the generations. For people who have been abused, simple affection can be difficult to give to their children. Those children then have difficulty with affection and so you see that the same affects of the sin from abuse has its affects down the generations.

When I began my journey of inner healing I discovered that the same wounds that had been passed to me through generations did not stop there. I realized I was in fact responsible for bringing the same kind of pain to the people in my family. This led me to become overwhelmed with grief. How can we prevent hurting our own children? The answer is we can't.

The only thing we *can* do is to continue to clean up our hearts. The cleaner our hearts become the more we can love those around us. It is like our hearts area chalice meant to be filled with water to quench our thirst for love and purpose. When we are wounded our hearts become cracked and the graces that God desires to fill us with leak out. We are barely able to contain enough grace to refresh ourselves much less share with others who thirst. This is where Christ's victory over sin comes in. The wounds on Christ's body were the consequences of our sin. Our sin created the wounds.

Venerable Archbishop Fulton Sheen said that he could see his own pride in Christ's crowned head, his own grasping for earthly things in Christ's hands, his own fleeing from the shepherds care in Christ's pierced feet and his own wasted love in Christ's pierced heart. Just as sin caused wounds in Christ's body so too does sin create wounds within our own hearts. At the resurrection, the wounds on Christ's body did not restore to unbroken flesh but became even more glorious because they became great signs of his victory over death and sin. When we allow Christ into our wounds, when we allow his healing power to wash into the cracks of our hearts, something extraordinary happens. Imagine you have a chalice to drink from but it is cracked allowing water to leak out of those cracks. You would not be able to quench your own thirst much less share with others.

Christ pours himself into the chalice and the effects are as if the cracks are sealed with stained glass. The chalice cannot only retain what fills it but also radiates light through the cracks so that all who are thirsty now know where they can quench their own thirst. Just as Christ's wounds became glorified, so too do our own when we turn away from the liar and call out to God.

We begin to radiate Christ through our most broken places because this is where we are small and he is big. The enemy wants us to hide these cracks. He wants us to hide our sin and the wounds we have from other people's sin. This way he can control us with fear of rejection, abandonment, and shame so we hide from one another. All we truly want is to be seen, to be known and understood and accepted and loved yet the devil convinces us to hide ourselves under the metaphorical fig leaf believing the lie that we are not lovable or redeemable. What a liar he is. "The truth shall set you free..."John 8:32

The reason why we are struggling in this world is not because we are somehow strange or because we are not faithful or pious enough, it is because we live in a world that has been divided by sin. Being faithful and growing in holiness can help us in our struggles but unless we address our wounds we may find ourselves carrying a larger struggle than God desires for us to carry by ourselves.

This is where inner healing begins. Healing begins when we understand how sin, lies, vows, and wounds work to separate us from God. I will use my own story to illustrate this so that you can expose the lies, renounce the vows and find healing in your own life. We all have a story to tell. It is in sharing that story that Christ is then radiated to others so they too can find healing. My desire is to show other thirsty people where they can go to quench their thirst. That place is Christ Jesus. He is the living water and when we drink upon His healing love, we will never be thirsty again.

HEALING THE "WHOLE PERSON"

"May the God of peace Himself sanctify you wholly; and may your spirit and soul and body be kept sound and blameless at the coming of our Lord Jesus Christ." 1 Thessalonians 5:23

"When we are fully joined to Jesus Christ, then we are able to be fully human." Resisting The Devil, Neal Lozano, pg. 12

The Center for Disease Control CDC says that 1 in 4 people are sexually abused. We are the walking wounded and many people are taking pills to numb the pain. Traditional therapy offers a clinical diagnosis as well as a psychological stigma for those seeking help to cope with the ramifications of growing up neglected, abandoned, traumatized and or abused. I have always known that traditional therapy was not the answer for me. The reason? It does not address healing for the WHOLE person.

We are body, soul and spirit. We must bring healing to our own "Trinitarian" being (in the sense of being body, soul and spirit). Traditional therapy either wants to give pharmaceuticals or just discuss and manage symptoms of anxiety, thoughts or behavioral issues or perhaps to do all three but not to actually bring healing and restoration for the "whole" person.

As a person who went to school for and earned a degree in Psychology, I have read many books regarding this subject. Some of the graduate courses I took in Family and Individual Counseling required us to see patients and we recorded the sessions to be critiqued as a class with our professor. Even then I was frustrated with the process of diagnosing instead of bringing healing.

It seemed like they were not teaching us to ask what the diagnosis meant. After all, we diagnose so we can bring healing and wellness, right? What traditional therapy does is diagnose and help cope with symptoms. What inner healing does is make the person whole, it heals them, just like we heal disease of the body, and it is my belief that inner healing can restore our person and our well being.

It is easy when we are dealing with a physical illness to desire a diagnosis. We see a doctor, get tests are diagnosed then treated. But what happens when you have an identity wound? You cannot get a blood test or take a pill three times a day until you are well.

Christ says He makes all things new. He promises us healing. Was He lying? Are we expecting too much? Are we giving the cross or God too much power? I say no. I say we do not expect enough. I believe Christ really has the power to work miracles. In fact, He worked miracles of healing and told the apostles that they would do all of the things He did and more! We are called to bring healing and deliverance to those in misery to be a sign of His power. Christ desires to restore us. Our healing is to be a visible sign to the world that our God is an awesome God and that He Reigns in Heaven and on earth. He makes us whole. I believe he wants to heal our emotions and our memories, not just our bodies.

We are called to evangelize and bring people to Christ. However, many of us are so wounded by sin (and the sins of others) that our lives are not exactly a billboard for Christianity. My life was no exception. I would try to "fake it" as best as I could. After all, the expression "fake it until you make it" was how I lived my life. But I was tired of the counterfeit. I wanted a double portion. I needed HOPE!

This realization motivated me to attend a retreat called "Healing The Whole Person" at a Catholic Parish in Florida. The day of the conference I walked from the hotel to the Church. I took my time getting there, as I was somewhat afraid of what would transpire once I got there.

When I arrived at the Church and made my way into what appeared to be an old cafeteria with a stage area, I took notice of a large statue of a saint on the main stage. I remember wondering who he was before finding a seat toward the back.

When the first opportunity to meet with one of the trained therapists came, I went up to the stage area to sit in a private area with him. As he led me through the process of uncovering the areas I was bound up in I was led to a re-occurring image in my mind of me in a crib I was crying and no one coming to me.

I did not think it was a real memory; rather it seemed to be a connection to a belief. It seemed to indicate a feeling of being neither heard nor having my needs met. This was an entry point of a false belief in which I had decided that I would make people see and hear me. I would control others to self-protect. Perhaps one of the most profound revelations occurred that day when I realized that someone could be both good and bad at the same time.

For me, I had put people in one of two categories; friends or enemies. There was no room for gray areas. I also was I introduced to finding my identity in the Father rather than trying to prove it or earn it. Having these three beliefs healed help free me and heal me.

When I sat with my second trained counselor and a nun from the Pierced Hearts of Jesus and Mary, something shifted. I actually felt something weird happen in my chest. The nun looked at me and asked me what I was experiencing as she was praying for me. I told her I did not know how to explain it. I told her it felt like my heart swelled up inside of my chest and stretched my rib cage.

In my mind I saw a picture of what I was feeling. I told her that the cartoon "The Grinch Stole Christmas" had a scene where his heart grew in his chest and he grabbed it and yelled out as it grew several sizes. I felt like my heart was growing in my body. I would have been worried that I was having heart palpitations or some kind of medical emergency but with this sensation I felt an infusion of joy and peace that felt like a deep sigh of relief.

She smiled and pointed to the large statue on the stage. Do you know who that is? She asked me.

"No", I replied.

"That is St. Philip Neri. He was a saint that experienced such a transformation when the Holy Spirit permeated him that his heart grew inside of his chest and swelled so large that it cracked one of his ribs. It was later confirmed after his death that one of his ribs did indeed crack."

I was blown away that this Saint, the one I have never heard of that just so happened to be the Saint over this particular parish, was present in the very place in which I was experiencing a great healing accompanied by some kind of physical manifestation that paralleled his own experience. I not only received a healing of my identity, but the Holy Spirit brought healing and restoration to my identity. I had a sensation that validated that my experience was very real.

I was not faking it. I was feeling it! I was infused with Joy and I felt like I had valuable. I was just "good" and I rested there absorbing as much of it as I could. It was my first taste of healing of what I now am certain were identity wounds that many therapist or psychiatrists would label as disorders.

We are not disorders. I believe many people who have been sexually abused or experienced traumatic childhoods like I did are actually dealing with identity wounds that distort their ability to know themselves and to know God. Being abused has a very real and powerful effect on shaping our identity. To merely dismiss that and label someone as being "disordered" is, in my opinion, causing more damage and in a sense, keeps their pain and cries for help unheard.

I realize we can categorize and diagnose and give our psychological disorders a name, but what good is it to give it a name if you do not understand it enough to help bring healing?

Many of our disorders come from identity wounds. How do we get identity wounds? We get them when our true identity is distorted by shame. It may sound contradictory to say there is such a thing as "good shame" but in fact there is good shame and bad shame.

Good shame is felt when we are separating ourselves from God as well as others in a selfish way. It "prickles" our conscience and in this way it helps us to address a something we are doing that we know is wrong so that we can self-correct. This "prickling" of conscience is from our awareness that we have just separated ourselves from what is good and true. This not only helps us shape our morality but it also protects our self-respect. When we feel "good shame" we become aware that we have lost our innocence, it motivates us to correct ourselves, and it turns us back to what we know is good.

Bad shame is more of an emotional torment and sickness to our very soul. It is what begins to poison and divide us from within our whole self. All of us have shortcomings. When shortcomings are used to ridicule us or to inflict "bad shame", we tend to believe the lie that we are bad or unworthy and this new "truth" sears into our heart, mind, and soul. We believe the lie that we are inferior, unworthy, undeserving, and bad to the bone. Bad shame causes us to despair, which separates us from our only cure to what ails us, which is God's mercy.

The inflicting of this debilitating shame comes from those closest to us and causes the deepest of wounds. When we are children, our beliefs are being shaped, especially our beliefs about who we are as a person. If the message we get is that we are bad or unlovable, it can become our identity.

Identity wounds distort our ability to love ourselves, to love others and to love or know God. Before I share with you the details of my own journey of healing of my identity wounds, I want to first explain the concept of identity.

When I was in Philadelphia for a course on Theology of The Body, the instructor used an example of our identity in God that continues to stick in my mind. He used the example to show the dignity of the body, but I want to use it as an example to describe the dignity of the person, especially that of someone dealing with identity wounds. He took a sheet of paper and showed us its flawlessness. It was without spot or blemish. He asked us to imagine that this was man and woman's goodness before the fall from sin. He then crumpled the piece of paper up into a ball.

I have felt that I was just like that crumpled paper. I believed for many years that I had to throw the paper out because I was no longer "good".

What I attempted to do was to recreate myself or hide myself from people. I had often done whatever I needed to do to be accepted or feel acceptable. What Christ did is He came and removed me from the trash and opened me back up. In doing this I, saw that I was better than just good, I was a gift. This lesson was given through the writings of Pope Saint John Paul II's (JP2) Theology of the Body.

The Theology of the Body is the term used to describe the teaching of Pope John Paul about the human person and human sexuality given during his Wednesday Catechesis in St. Peter's Square between 1979 and 1984. John Paul II called this catechesis "Human Love in the Divine Plan" or "The Redemption of the Body and the Sacramentality of Marriage." He did this by going through scripture and opening it up to understand it in a way I had never known before.

As a person who was sexually abused, I believed that what was done to my body was not done to me. Yet the reality is that it was. The abuse was done to my body and because my body and soul are intimately intertwined, the abuse affected my entire "person."

Man and woman were created for the sake of the other and find each other only in giving of themselves to each other as a gift. The human body was created to express love through the gift and to affirm the other by giving oneself to the other. The nuptial meaning of the body is our call to love and be loved in and through our body.

For years I believed that the body had nothing to do with God or love. I thought love was only a heart thing or head thing. The writings of Pope John Paul II have helped me understand that God desires to reveal himself to us in and through our bodies. To know that there is a sacramentality to my body, that it is a sign which makes the invisible personhood of Christina King visible to the world has filled my heart with joy. I am a marriage of the physical and spiritual and this is what makes up my whole person. Each of us are given a glimpse as to what our true identity is and how our dignity as persons created in His image and likeness is proof of our greatness and that glimpse comes through the writings of Pope John Paul The Great. I call him the great because his words have inspired me to reclaim my God given greatness. JP2 reminds us that man was not created as a hierarchy as if man was just a step up from animals. Rather God paused as if to "enter back into Himself" to make the decision to make man in His own image and likeness. (TOB 2:3)

Being a person means we are both a subject or "gift" as well as being in relation with an "other". It is not good for us to be alone, so God made man and woman and we are uniquely complimentary. Our bodies reveal that we are called to union and communion. Our bodies as male and female make visible that we are called to be a gift to one another in life giving love.

Sin distorted this image. Adam and Eve were naked without shame before eating the forbidden fruit because there was no need for shame in their original innocence. Only after Adam and Even sinned, or turned away from God separating them selves from truth, life and love did they feel shame and this shame caused them to cover themselves.

It is our fear of being exposed as well as our belief that we are worthless or bad that causes us to cover ourselves in shame. Good shame prompts us to turn back to truth, life and love. When we hide ourselves as Adam and Eve did we embrace the lies of the evil one and our identity becomes distorted.

In this distorted view it is difficult if not impossible to be in relationship with others. Our truth becomes subjective, our love becomes an object for use, and our lives lose their purpose and meaning.

Instead of dealing with our real issues, (identity wounds) we are being diagnosed with disorders. Ironically, the worse thing we can do to a person with identity wounds is to give them an identity as being "disordered".

Let's think about the word "disorders" through the lens of Theology of the Body. For something to be disordered it has to have been rightly ordered but then twisted. When Pope Saint John Paul II wrote about Original Man he reminds us that in Genesis that Adam was naked without shame. He had no desire or intention to use Eve as an object of pleasure for his own selfish needs or wants. They were both subjects of God and saw one another as persons. When sin entered the garden they were no longer seeing one another as subjects but as objects. They covered their "private parts" of their bodies in shame.

The good and right became disordered due to sin. This is the reality of the world in which we live. If this is true, we see we are all disordered in one way or another. If we are all disordered in some way, how helpful is it to give a person made in the image and likeness of God a label of being disordered as if this is their identity or who they are as a person? I am guessing it could be potentially destructive and could create further woundedness. Let's call disorders what they truly are, which is distortions of truth upon which we base our lives and relationships.

We are complex human beings. The teachings of Theology of the Body help us to understand a bigger picture as to who we are as persons and how we are made to love and be loved as self-gift whereas psychology bases "truth" in disorders or distortions.

Our experiences in and through our bodies shape our understandings and beliefs and those beliefs can bind us up or set us free. We act on our beliefs and if those beliefs are disordered it goes to follow that so too may our actions be disordered. For example, when I experienced the trauma of being sexually abused, it created a deep wound that penetrated my identity, distorting my whole person. Psychology may have helped me to understand the distortions and behaviors, but Theology of The Body helped me to understand my wounds and their effect on my identity. It was this distorted identity that shaped my beliefs and those beliefs caused me to make the choices in my life that I did.

Looking at someone's whole person, body, mind, emotions, memories, spirit, etc., is what needs to happen if we want a person to reclaim their greatness. Seeing the whole person as opposed to a disorder is what gives true hope for healing. Anything else merely treats a part of a person. Christ comes to make all things new, not part of things new.

During the years I was in conventional therapy no addressed the possibility of healing nor did they see me as a whole person. Instead I was a label or a diagnosis that was in need of new behavioral strategies or possibly medication to help me "cope" with the aftermath of abuse, neglect, and trauma. It is my belief that I suffered from a schism within myself, which put a wedge between God and me due to the traumas of my childhood. This schism distorted my perception of my identity as well as my ability to love and be loved by others. If love is a self-gift to an "other" then it makes sense that my distorted identity affected my ability to be in healthy relationships. Based on my experience and knowledge as a Psychologist, inner-healing has healed me from Borderline Personality Disorder and Emotional Deprivation Disorder.

There are many people dealing with identity wounds. It can be difficult to know whether or not your identity wounds or the identity wounds of a loved one are disorders or wounds. The next chapter goes through Borderline Personality Disorder and Emotional Deprivation disorder as they relate to my own identity wounds. I am going over these two in particular because I believe that I was healed from both of these "disorders." I will be referring to Borderline Personality Disorder as BPD from here on.

DESPERATE FOR LOVE:
Emotional Deprivation Disorder

"What if I could speak all languages of humans and of angels? If I did not love, I would be nothing more than a noisy gong or a clanging cymbal.

What if I could prophesy and understand all secrets and all knowledge? And what if I had faith that moved mountains? I would be nothing unless I loved others.

What if I gave away all that I owned and let myself be burned alive? I would gain nothing unless I loved others.

Love is kind and patient, never jealous, boastful, proud or rude.

Love isn't selfish or quick tempered. It doesn't keep a record of wrongs that others do.

Love rejoices in the truth, but not in evil.

Love is always supportive, loyal, hopeful and trusting....

For now there are faith, hope and love. But of these three, the greatest is love." 1 Corinthians 13:1-7, 13

The most common unmet need, in my opinion, is affirmation. Without affirmation we can never become the best version of ourselves. It is vital to our very existence as persons. Why? Because we are all so desperate for love that if we do not receive affirmation we begin creating a false self or persona. We become a chameleon and change ourselves to fit in to a situation so as to be liked or affirmed. Tina Turner's song "What's Love Got To Do With It?" could have been the mantra of my life. Love was a second hand emotion and I agreed with her, who needs a heart when a heart can be broken?

I learned to be what people wanted so they would like me. To this day I must resist the temptation to conform or hide myself. I read the book "How to Win Friends and Influence People" because I wanted to be able to control them and how they treated me or saw me.

Growing up I moved around so often I learned the tricks to make friends or identify the popular kids so I could join their lunch table. I compromised in more ways than one. I became sexually active at a young age and used my sexuality as another tool to find affirmation. What I did not realize was that I was not being affirmed and I most certainly was not being loved.

I did not know what love was. Instead I believed I was an object to be used. I needed to make sure I was always wanted so that I could believe I was valuable.

I have always been fascinated with Psychology. I majored in it in College and graduated with a degree in Psychology and even took some graduate courses in Counseling. I did this as yet another attempt to "control" my healing. Intellect was another false idol to me as a means to self-justify. If I was smart and could prove it to others, then they would have to like me. I was constantly in need of affirmation. I wanted to be more than liked, I wanted to be loved, but I had no understanding or real experience of the kind of love spoken of in the bible.

It had never dawned on me that *all* of us are worthwhile and valuable. We are all unique, unrepeatable persons and there is nothing we have to be or do to be given this dignity. It is God-given. Our parents are the ones that are to affirm us as good, valuable, and worthy of love without our having to earn it. If you grow up without affirmation you become emotionally stunted. There is a name for this and it is called emotional deprivation.

I first realized that I had symptoms of what is called Emotional Deprivation Disorder when I read the book, *Born Only Once* by Dr. Conrad Baars. It would be some time before I figured out how to heal the wounds it created in me.

FACING MY IDENTITY WOUNDS:
Borderline Personality Disorder

"Therefore if anyone is in Christ, he is a new creature; the old things pass away; behold, he is made new." 2 Cor 5:17

In the book, *Surviving a Borderline Parent; How to heal your wounds & Build Trust, Boundaries and Self-Esteem* by Kimberlee Roth and Randi Kreger, tell us that more women than man are diagnosed with Borderline Personality Disorder (BPD). They go on to say that there is conclusive research, which indicates a correlation between sexual abuse and the diagnosis of BPD.

But what if BPD is really just a fancy name for someone with severe identity wounds? What if these wounds have been left unhealed for so many years that the result is a schism or fracture within a person? What if those fractures are making them incapable of seeing truth, to live meaningful lives, or to love and be loved by others?

If our beliefs affect our behaviors then the DSM-III-R, which is a diagnostic and statistical manual used to identify and diagnose mental disorders, is a tool used by most psychologists. This tool uses 8 Criteria for diagnosing BPD based on those behaviors could be a tool to bring healing for persons with identity disorders.

The WebMD describes BPD as follows;

> *"Borderline personality disorder is a mental illness that causes intense mood swings, impulsive behaviors, and severe problems with self-worth. It can lead to troubled relationships in every area of a person's life.*
>
> *Most of the time, signs of the disorder first appear in childhood. But problems often don't start until early adulthood. Treatment can be hard, and getting better can take years. Problems with emotions and behaviors are hard to improve. But with treatment, most people with severe symptoms do get better over time.*
>
> *Experts don't know exactly what causes borderline personality disorder. Problems with chemicals in the brain that help control moods may play a role. It also seems to run in families. Often people who get it faced some kind of*

*childhood trauma such as abuse, neglect, or the death of a
parent. The risk is higher when people who had childhood
trauma also have problems coping with anxiety or stress."*

*http://www.webmd.com/mental-health/tc/borderline-personality-
disorder-topic-overview*

A person with BPD is someone without an identity in Christ. They are
unable to base their value and worth on truth. Instead they rely upon
others to shape their identities. The only one that can give us our
identities is God because He is truth, life, and love from an unchanging
source. The fact that it "runs in families" confirms my belief that you
cannot give what you do not have. If you were never affirmed and have
identity wounds, how do you affirm another? The answer is you can't
unless you are healed.

Many experts believe that trauma, abuse, or neglect result in an
increase risk factor for developing BPD. If this disorder is merely
identity wounds and if the Holy Spirit is the Divine Physician, then
perhaps BPD can be healed. The diagnostic criteria used in the DSM-V,
a test used by Psychologists to diagnose many psychological disorders
like BPD, can be used as a model in identifying persons suffering with
identity wounds.

In Dr. Kreisman's book he uses the DSM-III-R (diagnostic criteria of
borderline personality disorder, herein referred to as BPD) to define the
criteria of BPD. A person would need to be display the following
criteria 80% of time. What I found was that I could relate to almost all
of the criteria and had lived it out for most of my life.

I am going to go over each area outlined in the diagnostic criteria and
share which I exhibited as well as how I believed Christ healed me of it
as it pertained to my identity wounds.

Criteria 1: Splitting

Unstable and intense interpersonal relationships, marked with shifts in
attitudes towards others (from idealizing them, to devaluing, clingy
dependence, or isolation and avoidance), and prominent patterns of
manipulation of others.

It can also be referred to as "splitting". I did this. I did this to protect
myself. I put people in one of two categories: they were either good or

bad. I could not trust the bad people; I could trust the good people. If someone I believed was good hurt me, I did not see a good person making a mistake or doing something bad, instead they became bad in my mind. It served a purpose. It helped me to protect myself. It helped me to control my environment, my actions and my relationships with others.

My Identity Wounds and my splitting behaviors led to many unstable relationships. It was because of my inability reconcile the fact that people could be good and yet do bad things. Because of my identity wounds I made unrealistic demands on others and many times was referred to as being spoiled, which further injured my identity.

I have always had to ask others what they think because I valued they're input as being better than my own. My identity wounds created such a distrust of others that I have great difficulty trusting the motives of almost everyone I have ever met. This is because it provided me the only protection I felt that I had: if I could be proactive in determining who was safe and who was not, then I felt more capable of not being hurt.

Lack of BOUNDARIES

Boundaries assist in deciding to what we say no and to what we say yes. They are about how you separate yourself emotionally, spiritually, physically, intellectually, and even financially from others. Boundaries are important because it is how we learn to trust and how we move through levels of intimacy with people. What a struggle life can be when you see everyone you ever meet as a potential threat and have to evaluate them and categorize them before you can take the time and know them. That can result in extreme boundaries. I was making people objects and not seeing the person in front of me. This way of functioning caused a great loneliness, as no one was ever really be allowed in. There was even a process to determine if someone could be considered as a worthy of my trust. It was as if there were layers to intimacy with me and hardly anyone was ever allowed into the closest circle, the circle of trust.

I should note that boundaries are good. I am now learning to set healthy boundaries with people I meet as the remedy to compartmentalizing them. I now try to be open to everyone I meet and allow a natural friendship develop. Time-tested friendships are how we allow people to move through the boundaries to enter more fully into our hearts. This is healthy.

What I used to do was keep everyone out of my heart but share details of my life that should have been reserved for only the closest of friends who knew me. When I was rejected, I would see them as just another person who betrayed me or failed me. I never realized the part I was playing in causing so many friendships to crash and burn.

I still find myself watching people's facial expressions, keeping tabs on inconsistencies that may expose them as being inauthentic or untrustworthy. I am still growing in maturity in this area and I must constantly remind myself that this is a chink in my armor. I must continue to ask Jesus to help heal me of this mistrust. If I do not, it will only create greater loneliness and despair.

I had also noticed that I had become extremely dependent on my husband and my children. I wanted them to be with me but because of my fears, feelings of deep inadequacy and shame, I did not want them to touch me or expect too much intimacy. The guilt from feeling I was a bad mother would exacerbate the self-loathing. Intimacy is also a boundary thing and there are many levels of intimacy. For instance I am more intimate with a neighbor that tells me they have had a death in the family than if a stranger tells me the same. For me, boundaries were about how far into my life I allowed a person. and intimacy was about how much I allowed them to see of me. I had almost no boundaries and almost no intimacy.

Lack of INTIMACY

The word intimacy is sometimes referred to as In-To-Me-See. For someone with identity issues I wanted people to look anywhere but at me. The irony of this is that I longed to be seen. I was victimized, so I was very distrustful of people growing up, even by those who seemed to care. I believed the lie that they were only trying to manipulate me so I would let down my guard. Perhaps they just wanted something. Emotional intimacy was difficult, but physical intimacy was even harder.

I have never liked being touched. If my identity was distorted then the shame ran so deep it was as if I was untouchable as much as I was unlovable. If you cannot give what you don't have then, perhaps I was unable to touch and be touched because I had no source of love to share with others. I am continuing to work on this and have not found full healing here, but there are many days I am more capable of affection than others and that is a definite improvement.

For a person to find healing in this area they need to be deeply affirmed. In the chapter "Head and Heart Immersion" I share my experience with Charlie and how he was a catalyst in bringing healing to this area of my life. Dr. Conrad Baars talks about this in his book, *Healing The Unaffirmed*. Healing of persons who were never affirmed can only come from a person perceived as a father or mother figure. Charlie was old enough to be my father. He was there with his wife and yet I believe that when he affirmed me, he was affirming my inner beauty as well as my outer beauty. I could believe him when he told me I was beautiful. I allowed his compliment to penetrate my heart like never before. I was healed by his loving and affirming words.

Criteria 2: Impulsiveness

Impulsiveness in at least two areas that are potentially self-destructive, i.e. chemical abuse (tried that), sexual promiscuity (check!), gambling (not so far but only because I knew to stay away), shoplifting (yes), excessive spending (still fighting this one), overeating (did it say only two? Cause this makes four), anorexia nervosa (no self control for this one) or bulimia (so now I am at five areas).

To be considered impulsive, one must score a 'yes" on two of the areas listed above. I can list five. Impulsiveness is a strand and sudden reaction to how one perceives a situation, resulting in repetitive mistakes. I have always been proud to refer to myself as someone that *flies by the seat of my pants*. The need for immediate gratification and absolutely no patience has attributed too much of my impulsiveness.

The lack of self-control continues to cause idolatries or false gods in my life. Substances become a comforting idol. I become slothful when I am overwhelmed. I buy things to make me feel better. I find I still get angry over the simplest of things but I now realize that this is a distress symptom that should catch my attention so I can discern what triggered my identity wounds.

TRIGGERS

We all have triggers. We all have a chink in our armor. Certain things people say or do can be triggers. This is even truer for someone with BPD. When this happens the result is that we are feeling the hurt of our wound and we turn to our false gods in an attempt to self-sooth. I now realize I must go to the God the Father and check in with Him first to be affirmed and know who I am in His eyes and receive His mercy. Only then do I look at why I am upset. I am usually triggered by an old belief that I am bad, selfish, manipulative or undeserving of love or happiness. Another common trigger is feeling that I am not being heard, which then triggers feelings of not being valued. It is important to start identifying the triggers in our lives. The triggers are what set us off running away from God. The triggers are what pull us back inside of ourselves and the result is our distress symptoms (see Wound Chart in Appendix C).

This personal awareness came from learning about the cycles of addictions as related to shame taught by Dr. Bob at my very first course, which was called "Sexual Healing and Redemption". It was also in his teaching of the connection between our sin, the idols we turn to because of the lies we believe, the vows we make to self-protect rather than go to God, and the root wound that triggers it all that truly allowed me to expose the lies in my heart.

Because I have a degree in Psychology, I have gained a great awareness of how we think and feel and then observing behaviors as a direct result. I always loved Dr. Phil's comment, "You can't change what you won't acknowledge." It is for this reason I have always looked to the why behind what I do. The problem was I was always dealing with my sin or living out of the wound. When we live out of a wound we never really realize we are wounded, how it triggers us, and how we use things or people as false gods to help us control the pain, ignore the pain or deny the pain.

When I lived out of my wounds it was like I had a filter that interpreted what people were saying. Instead of someone saying, "I won't be able to come over today," I would hear, "I could come over but don't want to because you are not valuable." When I could not control things around me, I would rage to protect myself and use excuses to remain a victim, or I would come up with things to blame on other people as to why they were rejecting me or why I did not care.

As a youth, I would use self-destructive behavior to cope or release some of the pain. This would create guilt, which in turn caused more shame. I then would seek out a substance to numb or comfort myself. It is as if we know that sin deserves to be punished and our wounds convince us we ARE our sins and so we punish ourselves. The devil brings us 99% truth (always without the merciful love of Jesus Christ) and 1% lie and this is the rope by which we hang ourselves. Learning the relationships between sin, lies, vows, and wounds has helped me to identify when I was being triggered. It was something entirely different that gave me healing in this area. We are not our sin. We are not the identity our family gives us. We are sons and daughters of Christ. We are precious.

One morning after getting the kids off to school I was watching a woman televangelist by the name of Joyce Meyers. She said something that hit me right between the eyes. She said, "When the devil comes to tell you what a sinner you are and remind you of all the things you have done and why you are unworthy of being saved, tell him that God knew what He was doing when He made you. You are no surprise to God. You are not Holy Ghost Jr. He knew you would fail Him and yet He created you anyway. If Satan has a problem with you, tell Him to take it up with God." I had never considered that before.

Wow! It's true! It's not like God is watching my life play out like a sitcom and when a new episode airs he shouts out "What was I thinking?" God loves me and He knew me and knew my name and knew when and where to bring me into existence. God wants me. He wants you too.

The book "*The Reed of God*" by Caryll Houselander was another crucial step in this process of healing. In the words of Caryll Houslander, "Out of all of the potential souls God could have created, God chose to create you!" I came across the book by accident, if you believe in such things. I love art and was looking her up online because she did the art for a booklet I had that used pictures to teach the faith to children. Her chapter titled "Emptiness" reminded me that the circumstances of my life formed me. Our form reveals our purpose or the unique way in which we are to be a gift to the world. Some of us are formed like a chalice; gold is hewn from the mud, forged in fire and beaten by a hammer to create our shape. A chalice holds the precious blood of Jesus and is used in the Holy Sacrifice of the Mass. Many of us were formed in this way and our form is the best way in which to be filled so we can offer Jesus to others.

I have exhibited at least five of the above indicators for triggers. I have tried to control everything, even my healing. I now realize that control is a false idol to cope with feeling powerless or being afraid I will be abandoned and alone. When I am unable to be in control, I am anxious and angry and either have a panic attack or act out in rage.

I believe that panic attacks can be another symptom of identity wounds. They are distress symptoms of feeling powerless and alone. Yet we are never alone for God is with us. We are not just some nameless person. Each of us is sons and daughters of the most high King.

My identity is in God the Father and by virtue of my baptism I have been adopted as His daughter. I am a daughter of the highest King. I am not a mistake. I am not my identity in my family, I am not an identity in my sin, I am Christina and my name means Christ Bearer. The fact that my married name is Christina King is not lost on me. It is a daily reminder that I am indeed royalty. Christina King, like Christ the King. Even our names were inspired by the Holy Spirit and I have made a hobby of helping people see that their names has within it the very truth of how they are called by God to be a gift to the world.

Criteria 3: Anxiety, Depression & Self-Pity

Radical mood shifts can include depression, irritability, and anxiety lasting either a few hours to a few days, although rarely. The person with identity wounds bounces between enthusiastic periods of energetic creativity to unproductive morbid self-pity and depression, blaming his or her failures on others.

I have always been told I was moody. I feel anxious and irritable when I am being assaulted, but now it is less often and not such a huge shift. If you combine this with a victim spirit it can feel and be very oppressive. What I mean by victim spirit is that people who act as if they are always a victim may not just have a belief that convinces them of this but a demonic spirit can also come to minister to this lie. A victim spirit enters with the lie that a person is a victim and helps to keep a person bound up there. You can see it in people who are always complaining about what is being done to them and how bad their life is. They are always lamenting about one thing or another and they are always without fault (in their minds).

I have tried to identify what triggers me. Tone of voice can be huge. When someone's identity is fragile, tone of voice can feel like a lashing rather than just a simple question. The guilt and shame go so deep that often words can trigger a person who has been assaulted by the same or similar words in childhood.

The other reason my moods would change would because I was hearing something that was not being said. I would hear people speak and assume something they said was a passive aggressive attack on me in some way and I would try to self-justify. Self-justification is a huge indicator of identity wounds and is linked to pride and making "self" our god. Our control of who we say we are becomes the god we go to rather than God, our Heavenly Father.

In my attempts to justify myself, I came across as bragging, being pretentious, or just downright rude and full of myself. When my family tried to express legitimate needs, I would self-justify. They believed their needs were not important to me and that I just did not care. Contrarily, there would be episodes of self-pity in which I believed I was a victim and I made sure to let everyone know how I was suffering under the unfairness of life.

As I found more healing and as I learned to trust God more I found that I could hear what people were saying rather than what my distorted identity was allowing me to hear. I also notice that I am much gentler with myself and do less "should-ing" all over myself. I realize I am not the fourth person of the Holy Trinity and so I am going to fall short. I am called to faithful not to be successful. This gives me hope.

CONTROL

By now you are noticing a theme. My nemesis was control. My healing of this came when I begged Jesus Christ to heal me of the spirit of control. I was using the above things to control the pain, to control my happiness, or to control how valuable or worthy I was. I was making an idol of things to replace God because I did not know God and did not know He love me just as I was. I did not have to fix myself before I could come to Him. I was finally able to do this was when I renounced control. I asked forgiveness from God and then renounced the enemies hold over my life.

I took authority in Jesus' name and renounced the spirit of Control, the name of the spirit who tried to consume the hope God gives me. God began to uncover the lies I had allowed to be sown in my heart about what being vulnerable meant. As He did, I became less fearful and more trusting. Once I realized vulnerability was strength, I was more capable of opening myself to those around me. I was finally able to hear what people were truly saying to me and I could stop justifying my value. . I could forgive myself when I fell short as long as I went to God the Father to affirm me in my identity. This was probably the biggest deliverance of my entire healing process. Forgiving ourselves is another step in healing our whole person.

Criteria 4: OUTBURSTS

Inappropriate and intense outbursts of anger can cause someone with identity wounds to have unpredictable and frightening behaviors that are disproportionate to what triggers them.

The underlying fuel of the rage is fear and guilt of disappointing someone and fear of being abandoned. It is so intense and so easily invoked that often spouses or children receive the brunt of this rage. The irony is that the fear of intimacy is a cry for help. The person with identity wounds pushes away the people they need most. They may even rage against their therapists, testing their commitment to stay.

One pattern of behavior I have identified is that when I have been met with repercussions for inappropriate behaviors I have always raged. I have said before that rage is another indicator of identity wounds. Anger or rage may be the sin, but the false god is control and the wounds we are trying to escape from may be the feeling powerless or abandoned.

It is as if deep down that place that St. Augustine speaks of as "knowing we were made for God" screams out against the lies and self-loathing and says "I am good". The story "*Horton Hears a Who*" by Dr. Seuss comes to mind. I imagine that place deep inside where we know we are a person is yelling out "I am here! I am here!" The Mayor of Whoville yelled out, desperate to be heard. That voice was calling out from within my very soul and just as desperate. I believe the rage is a self-protection of that one tiny shred of hope and truth that remains written on our hearts. Rage is the attempt to protect that truth.

My identity wounds caused me to misinterpret the motives, intentions, and even actions of those around me. I would believe they were attacking what little shred of goodness I was managing to hold on to. Rage was about forcing them out and protecting my shred of goodness, all of which would be lost if I did not have control. The only alternative I could see was that if they were right, then I was bad. I just could not live with that.

When I was not able to control someone or my environment, the anxiety would get so intense that I would either rage or attack. I would get so intense that everyone around me would back away and look at me as if I had lost it. In fact, I had. The intense emotions would rise up so fast and so strong it felt like a tidal wave rising up and engulfing me. It was sink or swim. To sink meant to look at what was happening and why I was reacting and that felt like drowning. The reason is I did not have mercy to help me see myself without prejudice or fear. To see I was wrong would mean I was bad. That was my lie. I could not reconcile good and bad. A person was either one or the other they could not be both. The truth is we are all good. God loves all of us. The bad is sin not the person. If our identity is not our sin but our identity in Christ then we are priests, prophets, and kings. The bad, the sin, is from the evil one.

I could not separate out the sin from the sinner. Since my truth was people's identities were based on being good or bad, then that applied to me as well. I continued to fall short and sin so I was always fighting against the belief that I was bad. I had no mercy for anyone much less myself. I continue to smile at the ironies that I was controlling, but out of control. I wanted to be seen but did not want anyone to see me. I was terrified at being alone, but I pushed people away.

As I said previously, I used to have many issues with this but I believe I no longer rage. I do still feel anger over the littlest of things at times, but I am getting better at asking forgiveness from my children or husband and to owning up to things I did or said that were not loving or fair to them. It has taught me an aspect of humility that allows me to love myself more when I do things that are not Christ-like. If grace perfects our nature, then I must be able to retain more grace, as I am growing more comfortable in my own skin.

I realize now that I do not have to feel bad about myself if I get angry. I can even feel angry with God. He can handle it and wants me to lay it all at His feet, even my anger. I still turn to food for comfort even though I recognize what gluttony is, a false god of substance to comfort me. It is another way in which I try to not be vulnerable and take what it hurting to God. Anytime we make a false god of something it is because we are not willing or able to go to God the Father. If this happens, we must ask him to reveal the barrier to us. We must ask His help to remove the obstacles with a prayer: "Come Holy Spirit and reveal the barriers to me, take away the obstacles that keep me from You."

Criteria 5: HURTING OURSELVES

Re-occurring suicidal threats, self-mutilating behaviors, or comments about dying soon or wanting to die are frequent ways to communicate the deep pain and are real pleas for help.

Self-mutilation (I am including excessive piercing and tattooing) is a sign of identity wounds. Excessive use of drugs and alcohol and even food are also means of self-mutilation. Looking back over the years, I have self-mutilated in many ways. I used alcohol and medication; I even used to pull the hair out of my head until vanity caused me to turn to cutting myself. I remember it make me feel powerful and not so weak. I also liked how it let me feel like I was taking the edge off of the latent anger and pain inside of me.

Some scratch themselves, cut themselves, or burn themselves. It is a form of releasing some of the guilt or alleviates some of the suffering they are experiencing internally. The reason persons with identity wounds self-mutilate could be to experience the endorphins the body releases during the mutilation (self-treatment for pain) or perhaps it is the soul's relief that now the hidden pain is being made visible in some way, uniting the body in expressing what the soul cannot express. Whatever the reason, this is a hallmark of identity wounds. This is Theology of the Body. Making the invisible visible! See me! See my pain! To manifest the inner pain in a physical sign on the body is to allow the "whole person" to express it consistently and to feel whole.

A person with identity wounds may get excessive tattoos or piercings. The way you will recognize a person who is self-mutilating with tattooing or excessive piercing is when you look at them and you cannot "see" their person. Instead all you see is are the tattoos or piercings. This is the body screaming, "You can look at me but don't "see" me.

Criteria 6: Self-Image

Identity distortion in at least two of the following areas: Self-image, Sexual Orientation, Long-term goals or career, Type of friends desired, Preferred values. I believe I have demonstrated how many identity wounds I have been dealing with over the years. Clearly I qualify for

MPD in these criteria. I have never accepted my own intelligence or attractiveness. I was taught early on that this is something subjective. I was taught my multiplication table by being quizzed and then slapped in the head when I missed one. I was yelled at and made to feel stupid. This is how the lie that "being smart" was something you earn and it is judged by how smart or stupid you are compared to others. This lie was my truth and I grew the sin of pride because I was always attempting to prove how smart I was.

I have struggled with my weight my whole life. I was told regularly (when I was getting too fat) that I needed to look and be a certain way. However, even if I would feel pretty, I would see someone prettier than me and then I would feel ugly again. My identity was graded on a curve and my value had to be proven or earned over and over again. The little bit of self-esteem I had gained through impressing others and was necessary and critical to love myself. I name-dropped; I bragged about who I knew and what I was doing all in an attempt to impress people so that I could love myself. My identity was in the hands of others and so it was a very fragile thing.

I believed I had to be someone people would like. I tried to be or emulate attributes that others had that I liked. I remember talking like a girl I went to school with and dressing like another. You name it and I would try it all in an attempt to find that perfection that would make people like me. I have driven many people away from my attempts to prove myself. I would use my accomplishments as proof of my value and herald it to others. My desire was to say, "See, I am valuable." That was viewed as others as, "Look at me! I am better than you!"

When others would share something they accomplished, I would immediately feel the need to protect my own value. I would attempt to prove how I was just as good or better in that area. I did not desire to hurt or wound them even though I inevitably did. I only wanted to protect my very fragile and subjective identity. Since finding some freedom in this area I have tried to go back to some of the people I did this to and asked their forgiveness for making them feel little or inadequate. This has not only been healing for many relationships, but it also has been freeing for me to see how affirmed I am when I do not have to earn or prove my worth.

Some people with identity issues frequently change their jobs, friends, and even life goals. Some may even change their sexual orientation.

Andrew Comiskey runs Desert Stream Ministries and lived as a practicing homosexual for many years before being healed of some very deep wounds that shaped his identity as a man.

— "Rejection is the flip-side of love; love in turn inspires us to love and accept ourselves. On this basis of personal security, we can look beyond ourselves to the needs and concerns of others. But if the acceptance doesn't translate to us, especially as it relates to gender and sexuality, our growth toward healthy relationships with members of both sexes will be hindered." Andrew Comiskey, *Pursuing Sexual Wholeness Guide*, 53

I never changed my sexual orientation but I did become very promiscuous, all in an attempt to find acceptance. I even explored many different religions and churches. Persons with identity wounds are more susceptible to joining cults because they are seeking unconditional acceptance. They want to be affirmed as good. This is the basic human need of every person but many do not get this, especially when neglect, trauma, or abuse is present in early childhood. This also can lead some into very destructive relationships of physical abuse. I have been in relationships that were abusive. I am grateful that I found the strength from God to leave them behind. Many do not. If you are one of those people, know that you are precious to God. There is nothing you cannot do with his strength.

I can do all things through Christ who strengthens me. Phil 3:14

Criteria 7: Emptiness

A person with identity wounds has chronic feelings of boredom or emptiness. They long and desire for purpose and without it some people with identity wounds chose to end their lives rather than face the feelings of emptiness and lack of purpose.There was only one time that I thought about suicide. I was in high school and had just moved back to live with my mother. I put almost a whole bottle of aspirin in my mouth but when I closed the medicine cabinet and saw myself in the mirror, I could not do it. I saw myself with a mouth full of aspirin and thought, "What are you doing?" I did not end my life but there have been many days where I stayed in bed and slept the day away unable to face my life.

I still have days where I am filled with a meaningless emptiness. Many of my pregnancies required months of bed rest. I went to a place of feeling like I would be better off dead. Those have been dark times for me. When you feel you have no purpose, life becomes very difficult and can feel empty. When you know God created you for a reason then you know there is a purpose to everyone's life, even our suffering has purpose when we unite it to God and go to him for the answer to the burning questions inside of us.

My greatest healing in this came when I read *The Reed of God, by Caryll Houselander* and realized the when we embrace emptiness we realize that emptiness is not without form or meaning. The reed by a babbling river is cut and whittled out with stops cut into and hollowed out. But when the creator blows his breath into the emptiness, lyrical music is played. The emptiness gives the reed its beautiful form from which to pour out its greatest gift, which is music. Each of us is formed in a purposeful way. We are either pounded into our shape like the chalice or perhaps the story of our lives may feel more like being cut and whittled. Maybe you feel like you were held to a hot fire and melted down before being poured into your shape. Still others will be formed by tender love like a nest is formed to the breast of the mother bird. Whatever the method, our shape is the perfect emptiness from which God desires to pour Himself into so to that He may play His lyrical music through us, or to sacrifice Himself through us or to bring a drink of Him to those who thirst. Emptiness is necessary or else there is no place for God. Without Him, emptiness is without purpose.

When we consider that our emptiness reveals our form, we can then have the courage to look at what shaped us as something most perfectly suited to reveal Him to the world. When we are small, He is big when we are weak, He is strong. Your form is perfect to receive Christ, conceive Christ within you, and bring it forth to the world.

Criteria 8: Alone, Alone, Alone

The person with identity wounds has such a problem with being alone that they seek out any means to fill the silence with whatever noise they can. If they believe their identity is relative to how others see them, to be alone would be to be without identity. Being alone exacerbates the feelings of neglect and abandonment.

This makes me think of the movie *Jerry McGuire*. The joke was he could never be alone…alone, alone, alone. This was his greatest fear. I am not sure why I have always been afraid of being alone. There are times even now when my children surround me and I think to myself, "I wish I had a moment to myself!" But when I am, it scares me to death. The thought of a silent retreat terrifies me. I have always put the radio on in the car or turned the TV on when no one is home. I have a really hard time with Eucharistic adoration for that very reason. The thought of going to a room and being alone, even though it is with Jesus in the monstrance terrifies me. It feels frightening. This is how I know I am not fully healed in this area of my identity. Fear is not of God.

I think it is because without the distraction of others I am exposed. I am terrified of what I will see and what God will say about me. I still forget sometimes that God does not come to strike us dead with lightening, but comes to restore us and raise us up to him. When we are small, we can go to Jesus and be lifted up in his arms to God the Father. I recently had another healing when I saw a picture on Facebook of a man hugging his daughter who joined a convent. It was a cloistered convent so he would not be able to see her again, she was saying goodbye. I saw this young girl in her father's arms and he was crying and she was crying but neither of them looked sad, it was more like tears of joy and pride and admiration and love. She looked small and he looked big and for this first time in my life I thought to myself, "If that is what it means to be small, I can be small like that." It is the lies of the evil one that, when believed, cause us to turn away from God. That picture undid a lie of what it meant to be little. The truth of what little looked like to me was that little means protected, held, safe.

I have even begun to look to the way in which my husband is such a beautiful father to our children as a means to reveal the love of God the Father to me. I can imagine God the Father being like my husband. He loves beyond measure, is playful and funny. There is nothing he won't dos for his children. There is no monster he would not fight, even unto death to protect them. My husband has been the biggest catalyst in my journey of healing because he has been the first person to show me what true love means and what it looks like.

I saw it for the first time when I was in labor with our daughter Sarah. I was in transition and a contraction came sooner than expected. I was not ready and panicked. As fear and pain gripped my body I realized I was not able to fill my lungs with air and as the contraction continued I thought I would pass out from lack of oxygen. All I could do was turn to my husband and grasp his arms, my face in a grimace as I tried to stifle the urge to cry out in pain. As I looked into his eyes I realized he was crying. His face was red, his lips were trembling and my first thought was why is he crying? I am the one in labor.

Then I knew. It was because he loved me. It was because he had entered into my moment like a musician enters his music and gives himself away in a solo. He entered into my moment and I knew that this man loved me. To see me in pain and be unable to do anything to help me or protect me had invoked a separate emotional response in him. He was in pain because I was in pain. I imagine that this is God the Father's heart for all of us.

I have many father wounds. This is still a place I am in need of healing. One of the last things I discussed with Dr. Bob was for me to ask the Father to reveal His love to me. I remember praying for God the Father to do this, to reach out in some tangible way and prove my value, my worth, and His care for me.

I remember asking for Him to make it a grand gesture. I felt that the hole inside was so great, my fear of Him so big that I did not want to miss whatever it was He would do to reveal Himself. I could never have anticipated the turn of events. In fact, it took many months for His plan to reveal itself and in the process, my faith and my healing were put to the test, but it was well worth it.

I believe that the healing power of Jesus Christ healed me of Borderline Personality Disorder. I am a new creation in Christ and know that Jesus can heal more than our bodies. He can heal our emotions, our memories, our very persons. All He needs is your yes.

"I am a handmaid of the lord be it done unto me according to your word." Luke 1:38

HOLIER THAN THOU

"It is Jesus that you seek when you dream of happiness; He is waiting for you when nothing else you find satisfies you; He is the beauty to which you are so attracted; it is He who provoked you with that thirst for fullness that will not let you settle for compromise; it is He who urges you to shed the masks of a false life; it is He who reads in your heart your most genuine choices, the choices that others try to stifle.

It is Jesus who stirs in you the desire to do something great with your lives, the will to follow an ideal, the refusal to allow yourselves to be ground down by mediocrity, the courage to commit yourselves humbly and patiently to improving yourselves and society, making the world more human and more fraternal."

— *Pope John Paul II*

Before I take you on my journey of healing, I feel that I need to expose a huge obstacle that had kept me from being healed much sooner. That obstacle is the spirit of religion. Knowing whether it was a real spirit or a tendency of my own heart to use religion as another means to control my life or whether it was a little bit of both does not change the fact that religion without relationship became an obstacle in my healing.

I had removed the metaphorical bandages and the wounds of my heart and they stank worse than I could ever have imagined. I had hidden them, ignored them, and made excuses for them for so long I had no idea how to heal them and without realizing it, this became my next big mistake. I was right to go to Jesus to find healing but I did not go to Jesus, I went to religion. I had made my faith a tool rather than a means of having a relationship with God. Once again *control* was operating in my life as I decided to use religion to *fix* my wounds.

The desire to fix myself should have been my first tip-off. I should have desired for my heart to be healed rather than merely fixed. I had no comprehension of how to heal my wounds or that such a thing was even possible, so I set about to fix them. I thought that religion had to be the way to do it! I was only partly right. What I discovered was that I was using religion to manage my life and cope with distress symptoms. I was still not healed. I was still not free.

My initial conversion came through the Miraculous Medal. This medal was cast in 1832 after the Blessed Virgin Mary appeared to Sister Catherine, a daughter of Charity. Sister Catherine Laboure of France received a vision or what Catholics call an "Apparition" of the Blessed Virgin Mary. In this vision she was told to have a medal cast of what she saw. The apparition was of Mary standing on a globe and holding a globe in her hands. From the precious gems set in the rings on her hands she could see dazzling rays of light radiating outwards. These were said to be the symbol of graces bestowed on all who ask for them. Around the image of the Blessed Virgin Mary the words "O Mary, conceived without sin, pray for us who have recourse to thee" surrounded her in an oval frame. On the back of the medal is the letter M, surmounted by a cross, with a crossbar beneath it. Under all of this were two hearts. The Sacred Heart of Jesus surrounded by a crown of thorns and the Immaculate Heart of Mary pierced by a sword.

I was given the Miraculous Medal and told the story of how many graces flowed to those who wore it and called upon Mary to go to her son and plead for intercession. It was through investigating her role in the Church that I was led to read of the story of Our Lady of Fatima and the selfless love of the three little children that told her story. It inspired me to believe that God was real. I began going to church and I learned to pray the Rosary. What I had not realized was that I was beginning to see religion as a way of controlling and manipulating God. I was using religion to fix it. I was not becoming holy; I was becoming holier-than-thou.

My husband and I had been married for about two years when the problems of family life as well as the baggage that came from my wounds (as well as his own) began to take their toll on us. My husband was raised Jehovah's Witness and had experienced his own abuse and neglect. He, too, experienced sexual abuse in multiple forms and because of adultery in his family he also shared in a dose of shame from being deemed a bad association, a term used for a family who had a member that was dis-fellowshipped.

Being dis-fellowshipped means the elders in their faith community publically declare that someone is too sinful to remain in good standing and is put outside of the faith. That person can no longer associate with the community. The humiliation of being reproved publicly and the isolation that comes from being put outside of the community can cause years of emotional wounding. My husband was horrified by this and was left feeling rejected and unworthy of friendship. He had used his own means of hiding his wounds with drugs and alcohol or by objectifying himself. All of these things were numbing agents.

We were a great pair and off to a great start. I say that sarcastically. The truth is, we were and are still a great pair. God knows what He is doing. Our spouse is like sandpaper. God gives us the perfect spouse. It can be painful, but ultimately, our spouse refines us. I was the outgoing and outspoken extravert; he was the quiet introvert that preferred not to be around people he did not know. I was the optimist to a fault; he was the pessimist in the same extreme way. He was 6'4" I was 5'2" but I always forgot how short I was and how big he was unless I saw us in a picture together. I have always felt much bigger than I am. My husband has even said once, upon looking at us together in a picture, "Wow you really are short. I forget how little you are." I think that is because for so many years I made him little, for so many years the controlling and dominating I did made me seem overwhelming and larger than life.

So here we were, dealing with real life issues with wounds that were causing us to react to one another rather than to see or hear each other and as a result more wounds were formed. In the beginning, religion became a really great gift, it gave me hope, it helped me to believe I was loved, it led me to repentance and change. Then, out of fear, I began to twist it into something that helped me control my future, my family and my pain. My husband had abandoned his dreams to work in a professional field and began working as a laborer to support our family. My own issues with being unaffectionate, controlling and emasculating were beginning to have its effect. I was a new convert and filling all of my spare time learning the faith and going to conferences. What I did not realize was that my husband, who was raised Jehovah's Witness, had his own wounds and I was like salt in them.

I heard Dr. Bob give an example of how our wounds were like having a broken arm. If I have a broken arm and you walk around bumping into my injury, it is going to hurt. That's what it can be like when we fail to see each other's wounds. Your words or actions can bump into my wounds.

Shawn's wound was a religion wound and I was becoming religious. I was more like a huge sledgehammer on his broken arm rather than just bumping in to it. There can even be a "Spirit of Religion" and I believe this was overtaking me. Religion is not by itself a bad thing, in fact religion is a beautiful and wonderful gift to the Church, but when it is disordered or encountered from a place of sin and brokenness, anything can become the opposite of the its intended purpose.

He had seen and experienced many things growing up, all in the name of religion. There were things that happened in his childhood that caused the congregation to dis-fellowship his father and henceforth deem his family a bad association. This meant that kids couldn't play with him or invite him over. People would give disappointed looks at the at meetings (worship services) rather than talk to them. He and the rest of his family would take their part in carrying the burden of shame along with their father for his actions.

At school, he was picked on for being in a weird religion. He was not allowed to participate in any holiday events and so he felt that religion not only set him apart from normal kids but it created an opportunity for persecution, judgment by others, and even potential abandonment, which he would experience later when his parents divorced. His parents divorced after almost 30 years of marriage. During those 30 years he suffered from neglect as well as circumstances that stripped him of his own innocence and purity of heart.

He believed that religion played the largest part in creating the circumstances that led up to the divorce. The lie he believed? "If Christina becomes religious, I cannot compete and she will chose her "god" over me. I will be judged, shamed, and eventually I will be abandoned by her." I should point out that there was some very legitimate fruits that growing in my faith brought us. One of those fruits was that I had begun to look at my wounds and desire to become less selfish, more loving and family orientated. The other was that my husband had decided on his own to go through RCIA, which is a program in the Catholic Church to catechize new incoming members.

We were quite the pair and we continued to bump into each other's wounds for some time before I would once again find myself crying out to God to save our marriage and heal me. In fact, my husband says that it was the changes in me that inspired him to desire baptism. He said I became less selfish. This change in me was what opened his heart to religion. I did become less selfish as grace began to flow into me, but I was still very much like a broken chalice. My wounds were like cracks and those cracks allowed any grace I received to leak out. I was hardly able to retain enough for myself much less to share any of it with others. You can't give what you don't have and I didn't have Christ, I had religion.

To make matters worse, we encountered problems in getting my husband baptized. It should not surprise us that the evil one would move hell and high water in an attempt to prevent someone from being baptized After going through the year long program, the priest informed my husband, less than a week before he was entering the Church, that he would not allow him to be baptized.

To say my husband was devastated would be an understatement. He swore off church and religion and it would be almost a year before he would ever step foot into a church again. There are many people who have been hurt by a representative of the Church. For my husband, it was the priest that denied him baptism and confirmation. My husband did not see a flawed man that let him down, he saw church letting him down and by default; God.

The sorrow on my heart was heavier than anyone could imagine. I had realized our marriage was not blessed, did not have God united in Sacrament with the two of us and now that he would not even go to church, I felt all was lost.

Another source of difficulty was his job. He hated it. Although he graduated with a degree from college, he continued to work in painting because it was a good income. The hours were awful, the benefits were non-existent and my husband's self-esteem, which had always been fragile, was crumbling.

I realized that unless we stepped out in a real way, he might always resent me. I am so glad I discerned this early on. We are all called to greatness and unless we are doing something that gives us passion and purpose in life, we will hunger, ache, and long for it. When we are wounded, we numb the ache rather than address it. We numb it with substance. St. Catherine Sienna says that if we are doing the thing God has created us for; we will set the world on fire with our gifts!

I knew that my husband had greatness inside of him and I wanted him to know it too. I am grateful that I loved him enough to want this for him rather than to love my wants and myself more. The extra work and financial strain created one cross after another. When we are devoid of grace, our cross feels like being crucified rather than transforming or life giving. My husband was so miserable that I felt I was losing him. He was always unhappy, he drank more and we were struggling with the teachings of Natural Family Planning. Not using contraception was a Church teaching that my husband felt he did not have to live by because he was not even allowed to be Catholic.

He threatened to get a vasectomy for years but he never did. The love in my heart swells up beyond explanation when I contemplate how much this man loves me to have remained open to life, to chasten his passions for love of me even though he thought that NFP was stupid and pointless. He did not believe in NFP or perhaps even in God, but he believed in me. He knew that if he did get a vasectomy, the love we had would be affected and possibly changed. This, he told me, was something he just couldn't risk. My husband is truly a gift from God, sent to help me work out my salvation. I can honestly say, regardless of the trials and tribulations we have had to go through, he is the perfect spouse for me.

I had met a woman named Lynn. She ran a Catholic bookstore from her house. We began to speak regularly. I started coming regularly to learn more and more about my faith and she seemed to have endless knowledge on all subjects. Eventually, she invited me to something called "Catholic Club" where we met over a 50 other families that were homeschooling, praying the Rosary and living what I guess could be called an alternative lifestyle. To me it looked like a faster way to fix what was wrong with our family and me.

Although Lynn has proven to be an exception to the rule, I have usually had a problem with keeping girlfriends over a period of time. She and I have remained friends to this day, are a real rarity for me, but there was another woman that I had become friends with that this would prove the case once again. One of the women I met at Catholic Club lived very close to our house. Her husband invited my husband to go to Eucharistic adoration. For those of you that are not Catholic, it is a prayer chapel dedicated to the presence of Jesus Christ. It can be a quiet place to pray to Jesus, to be filled, healed and restored. I was shocked my husband went, but he did.

This new friend asked me to start walking regularly and I said yes. We became friends quickly, as I often do, but very soon after it ended abruptly when she told me she just could not continue to be friends with me because the details of my childhood and my life were creating so much pain in her that she was up at night weeping over the details. This is a perfect example of how I did not establish appropriate boundaries. Even though I did not know her very well I shared very intimate details of my life with her on those walks. I shared the traumatic events of my childhood and because I have become desensitized to the details of my own life and because I had not learned the importance of boundaries, I passed through the levels of intimacy too quickly. When we make friends we become closer and share more intimate details with them over time. Trust is something that is earned.

I had not learned that. Instead I shared everything with everyone equally. If they stayed they were "good" and if they rejected me they were "bad." Her rejection of me did what all rejections did to me. It caused more cracks in my identity. I did not understand she was not rejecting me but was overwhelmed with the details of my life. Any normal person would be overwhelmed with hearing the details of my life. Because I had not yet learned this, I believed her rejection was of me giving further proof that no one loved me or could love me and that I was bad somehow. I could only stay in that "place" for so long. Then I would self-protect by moving into anger. I could either accept that I was bad or get angry and tell myself she was the one who was bad. That is what I did. I told myself she was a hypocrite, a terrible person, and an awful friend.

"Who does that? What right does she have staying up nights crying about my abuse? Is she serious? She must have mental problems and I am better off without her." These became the lies I told myself so I could make sense of her rejection and abandonment.

The alternative was that I was the one with the problem. Once again, I realized that while I desired friendship, I seemed to be incapable of making or keeping friends. Things went on this way for some time and family life continued to get worse. God made us for union and communion. When we walk around with wounds, we cannot truly see each other. This keeps us isolated. I have lost many good friends over the years because the pain they caused me felt too great. I never realized that it was not they that caused the pain; it was the lies I believed that hurt me.

I went on living this way for some time. We had five children by now but our difficulties were still escalating. I continued to manipulate and control my husband's conversion, our family, and possibly even God. I felt as if I was fighting imaginary dragons all of the time. It was exhausting. Although I had become aware of my wounds, after all I had ripped off the bandages in an attempt to deal with them, I was still not bringing healing to them. Instead, I was operating out of my wounds. Control was the way I dealt with anxiety and managed my pain. Religion was a neat little package of control. I was using it to do what I always did, hide the wounds and give myself a new identity.

I stopped wearing make-up; I got rid of all my pants in exchange for skirts and began to make my entire life about the Mass, Rosaries, novenas, and homeschooling. I did these things because I believed doing them would make me holy. I am not saying these things are bad, in fact is very good to go to Mass and pray the Rosary. These were the very things that helped me to enter into true conversion and repentance. To this day they are the means from which I continue to receive the necessary graces to perfect my nature. However, I was using them as if they were themselves "things" to use to achieve the ends of which I had desired. I was using them to control God. In fact, the changing of my wardrobe and the homeschooling was only so I could control my identity and not out of love for my children, to become humble, grow in holiness, or be authentically feminine.

The choices I made and the manipulation of religious things were all attempts at fixing myself and fixing my husband. I became even more discouraged with myself as I sensed the hypocrisy within myself.

That's when I began hiding my failures. I couldn't tell my friends any of my struggles because then I would lose value. I pretended that I loved it all and was doing great. All of this was, of course, far from the truth. We cannot change what we will not acknowledge. Yet I kept things hidden away in my heart and it began to harden as a result. To make matters worse, I had been going to a spiritual director that told me that I was too attractive to wear pants and must start wearing only dresses. This perpetuated the shame in side of me that the abuse I suffered was my fault. Had I been an unattractive child, perhaps I would have been left alone.

Some of the women I befriended had some peculiar ideas about religion. I was told women were objects of sin and if I wore make-up I would attract men. I was told if I wore pants men would lust after my body so I needed to offer up wearing pants as a penance for being attractive. This was of course puritanical thinking. It was the Manichean heresy that the soul and spiritual things are good but that the body is bad.

My husband began to get more and more concerned because I no longer looked like the woman he married. We went to a Mass that was in Latin and it was twice as long as our other Church. He continued to go because he loved me but he was becoming more concerned with the direction I was going.

When I look back and see how I abused this poor man with control, I see how I was my own worst enemy. I realize how all of that control caused so much pain and suffering in his heart. He did not want to lose me so he allowed me to be controlling out of his own fear of abandonment. He numbed himself more and more during this time of our life. The enemy is good at using our wounds as a means to destroy our marriages when the truth is that God has given us the perfect person to help us get to heaven. It is not always without pain or suffering. Even sand must be put into the fire before it can become crystal.

The sin of pride rose up within me as a means to protect my identity. I was speaking often at Catholic Conference and events and my feeling self-importance grew with every new speaking engagement. I signed on with one of the largest Catholic Apologetics apostolate in the world and was writing articles that were published in magazines, books, and even my own Diocesan paper.

That is when the turning point came. Sometimes the most excruciating circumstances create the most effective change. If you pray for humility, expect to be humiliated. God gives us what we need, not what we want. I had begun to pray for humility and God gave me the opportunity to learn humility.

I was booked to speak on EWTN. This is considered to be the Hollywood for Catholic Speakers. I was going to be on two separate shows while I was there. I was also scheduled to speak at a large youth event at a National Shrine. That is when it happened. My pride rose up one day and when I was on the phone defending myself to a woman that I had slighted, I name-dropped someone to show her my self-importance and that was the beginning of the end.

The next thing I knew, someone called EWTN and told them I was not authentically Catholic, taught sex education and promoted birth control. They got one of the two rights. I was not authentically Catholic. I am not sure anyone can live out his or her faith perfectly. I was trying, but I was failing miserably. After all, it was my way to control my wounds and feel better about myself but I was not letting my newfound beliefs to penetrate my heart.

So they cancelled my shows because they did not have enough time to investigate the allegations. I then received a call from the Shrine saying that they were told if I presented at their conference the youth ministers from several parishes would not allow the students from that Diocese attend. It was like a bad dream. Things went from bad to worse. My husband lost his job, my ministry was falling apart and the people I thought were our friends began to attack my ministry work and our family life. We were pregnant with our fifth child. When I reached out to our friends for support they told us that we should give our baby up for adoption.

I felt like I was having a mental breakdown as I watched everything fall down around me. I was completely overwhelmed. Religion was not cutting it. The good news is that sometimes God takes something apart before he rebuilds it stronger and better then it was before. I was beginning to feel the legalism of my religious friends. I was beginning to see that some of them where Pharisee. They knew the rules, they were great at knowing right from wrong and telling me what I should and should not do, but there was not a whole lot of mercy. If there was, I did not see it.

I felt the judgment and the hypocrisy of saying they loved Jesus but when Christ put me in their life, they chose to black ball me, print letters in the paper accusing me of things I was not guilty of, and ruining my good name, all of which are not Catholic much less Christian. Once again my husband decided that if the very people who are supposed to love us the most persecute us instead, that he wanted nothing more to do with any of them or religion. So we did the only thing we could think of to do. We sold our house and moved away.

There was so much I still did not understand at this point in our life. It would be quite a while before I would "get it" and there would be a lot more suffering along the way. This time, we would all share in the suffering, our kids included. It is how our wounds spread to others. We wound others because of our own wounds. I had felt neglected because of the selfishness of those who raised me. Now I was neglecting my own family. I was placing my own needs and wants before the needs of my children.

Then it happened that the lies were exposed and the tomb was opened. When it did I ran into the light.

HEAD AND HEART IMMERSION

"Wounds caused by a lack of love, or a distortion of love, are often at the root of our brokenness. That's why we call it 'healing broken hearts' ... healed by a positive experience of love. It is not enough to discover the roots of the conflict. We must fill the emptiness with the merciful love that flows from the heart of Jesus."

— *Fr. Emiliano Tardif, Jesus Lives Today,* page 73

It was through the teachings of Pope Saint John Paul II writings called *Love and Responsibility* and *Theology of The Body* that I discovered the path upon which my heart would be healed and transformed. It is through his writings combined with inner-healing and deliverance ministry that I would be made new.

To be precise, I attended a course called Love and Responsibility being taught by Dr. Janet Smith. It was held in Philadelphia at a retreat center for an entire week. I had never done anything like this before. I was attracted to it because it had an academic appeal to me. I believed I was going to be educated in an exclusive program that hardly anyone else was going to and this would make me valuable and elite. I had always admired Dr. Smith and looked forward to meeting her, as she was somewhat of a celebrity in my mind.

At this time in my journey toward healing, I was still the author of my identity so this course was a way in which maintained that I was valuable because I was growing in knowledge and status. Status was an idol to me because I still was not able to trust God with my life. What I failed to notice was that the courses were all designed to be for the head AND the heart. It was a course and a retreat experience in one so that our whole person would be engaged. We would not just learn about truth, life, and love, we would have an intimate encounter with truth, life, and love.

This retreat center engaged my head and my heart. It gave me truth but also opened my heart to understand what love is and what love is not. The irony was that my heart would experience a miraculous healing in a day's time but the knowledge of trusting it so as to grow in maturity would remain elusive for a few more years. My healing began when my wounds experienced an immersion of truth, life, and love through my head and heart experience of Theology of The Body Institute.

I heard it explained once that inner healing is like having a broken leg miraculously restored. It is healed but you cannot go run a marathon on it. It does not mean the leg is not healed, it just has not been strengthened and the healing has not yet matured. Healing truly can be immediate. Total healing usually is not immediate, but healing of wounds can be. When we find freedom in an area we did not have before, that is healing. We can walk but most probably cannot yet run. That does not mean the healing we experience was not real.

> *"A person's rightful due is to be treated as an object of love, not as an object for use."*
>
> — *Pope Saint John Paul II, Love and Responsibility*

My first lesson would be one of love. It would be the kind of love we call Agape. It was love of neighbor. I realized that my own past of physical, emotional, and sexual abuse had tainted and distorted my understanding of self-worth as well as my ability to show and receive love but what I did not know was that I had created some powerful strongholds when I used religion as a means to control my worth and did more damage than one would realize.

It was the second or third day and we were discussing how male and female God created us. We discussed how we are a unique creation and that as male and female we compliment on another. We continued to speak of how men find the feminine attractive and women find the masculine attractive and that this attraction is not sinful but is ordered for we were created by love for love. For love to exist, there needs to be a lover, a beloved and the fire of the love between them. Since we are created in the image and likeness of God, then when we are attracted to the opposite sex, we are in fact attracted to love and attracted to God. We dissected 'attracted' and it was said that attraction and lust are not the same. I had never heard this before and thought these people must be crazy.

I had always believed, that once attracted, that very same pull, that sensation of delight that I called attraction was, in fact, very sinful and the birthplace of lust. I believed that when you feel that pull or that attraction it must be stopped at its very first inception. in fact, if you could prevent it entirely it would be even better. This is why I wore dresses and not pants or short for so many years, so as to not attract or be an object of lust and occasion of sin.

I raised my hand and asked the question that was burning in my heart. "I have found that I find men very attractive. What I mean to say is, when I look upon men, no matter who they are or what they look like I find myself attracted to some part of them that comes from their masculinity. It may be there broad shoulders or the fact that they are so tall. It might be a timber to their voice, but whatever the thing is, I feel a warm sensation of butterflies in my stomach that feels it will float into my throat. It is almost a feeling like a sigh. I have always believed that this was very wrong of me. I believed that I must have some inordinate desire that stemmed from a childhood of abuse. I have believed that this *delight* in the opposite sex, has most likely been some kind of emotional dysfunction that I must try and *fix* or overcome lest I fall into sin."

I am not kidding when I tell you that most of that room looked at me with smiles like they understood what I was saying and yet still believed that attraction was not sinful. I went on to explain myself. I shared how I had learned to close myself off that I had trained myself to avoid eye contact with men that I did not know. If they looked at me, I certainly did not smile at them for that would be opening myself up and would make me vulnerable. I also believed that it would be leading them to sin because I would be then sending a message of interest and that would be wrong since I am married.

Imagine my surprise when I was met with an overwhelming response that my delight was not sinful, but rather it was the essence of Pope John Paul's message. That stamped into our bodies is God revealing the mystery of love and he desperately wants us to understand this!

There was a man and wife at the Seminar. His name was Charlie. They had been married for over 40 years. At one point he stood up and said to me and to the group that he thought I was beautiful and attractive. In fact, he went on to tell us all how beautiful I was and how it gave him joy to see me every day and that he took delight in seeing how beautifully feminine I was.

I began to cry. Why? Well, first of all it goes back to Dr. Conrad Baars' theory that to receive affirmation, it must be from someone that you believe is authentic as well as a from someone in authority.

If he had been a handsome young man, I would have made sure to sit on the other side of the room from them on. I would have avoided eye contact as well as conversation except for brief polite greetings. I would never have allowed myself to be alone with him, not even in Eucharistic adoration for that would have been too distracting to me. But, because he was sitting next to his wife when he said it, and was at least 30 years my senior, I believed him. I believed him so completely that tears streamed down my face and I could not stop them. I believe that one moment of understanding opened a floodgate of healing in my life.

I received healing, immediate healing, and freedom. I mention this because it seems to me so many of us are hurting from past abuse and we do not realize that we need smiles, eye contact, and yes, even touch because all of us need to be affirmed. We need to know that we are good just because. We don't have to do something or be something, we are good just because we are.

Touch is another huge wound for me. In fact, for so many years I had so much difficulty being physically affectionate. Touch felt like being violated. I could hug and kiss my babies, but right around the age of 5 or 6 I began to resent being touched and tried to avoid it. I had no idea what non-sexual physical affirmation was.

I did not receive regular hugs and kisses. I did not hold hands with my father or have him rub my back or move the hair from my face. I did not get squeezes of affection from my parents, as they would walk past me at home. Affection felt more like chewing glass. I could be sexual, if it was in the bedroom I could be affectionate, but even that was either rare or I had a hard time with kissing. It is an intimacy thing. I felt that is was more intimate than even having sex.

One of the presenters, Christopher West, mentioned the Manichean demon and heresy. This is the name of a heresy that taught that the soul was good but the body was bad. He talked about how it is not sinful for a man to look at a beautiful attractive woman and see her, smile at her, and say to himself, "That is a very attractive, beautiful and feminine woman." In fact, he mentioned that it affirms a man in his own masculinity to see his feminine counterpart and delight in her being created as feminine. He wasn't talking about lust, he was talking about recognizing that woman is a beautiful creation and sight to behold and her creation as woman is a delight!

I had NEVER thought about this concept. Suddenly, I realized that the very need to be loved that I have been carrying around with me was starving me emotionally. I had bought in to a lie that my body was something that would lead men to sin and could not be trusted. I believed that if I even smiled at a man I would be inviting him into an occasion of lust. I had even begun to fear confession. I worried that if a priest heard me speak about anything to do with sexuality, that I would be scandalizing him for surely he would have lustful thoughts about me.

My twisted understanding of the body had begun to distort my image of masculinity. I had begun to believe that all men were easily tempted and would be led to feelings of lust with even the slightest of provocations. This of course distorted how I believed my husband felt about me. I believed all of the times he reached out to give me affection he was just trying to use me, objectify me, or was lusting after me.

I do not say this to sound as if my looks would tempt any man but rather to point out a flaw within myself. For one, past abuses that I had encountered had trained me to keep people at arm's length, for my own safety and for theirs. Two, the über Catholic groups I had encountered had presented the same theme. I must say that this lie and judgment had led me to believe that my body was an obstacle to my own holiness as well as the holiness of others.

After that night, I decided that whenever I saw someone look at me and make eye contact, I would hold that gaze for a moment and smile with all the love in my heart that I could. I would think the words, "God loves you." When I left the Institute and arrived at a Philadelphia airport I was on a mission. I decided that if I saw a man look at me, I would smile with love. One after another I made eye contact and smiled when I felt someone's eyes on me. I cannot describe the joy in my heart that I experienced with the events that followed. I remember one man even tipped his hat. I did not see lust, I did not see invitation, I saw warmth and an almost thankfulness behind their eyes.

I came to realize that we all desire to be loved and accepted. It is in our daily activities that we can give and receive love. We can do that by looking upon one another and delighting in their creation and saying you are beauty to my eyes! I delight in your creation!

We need to overcome the heresy that the body is an impediment to holiness. It is this heresy that I believe to have been my own obstacle in believing in and accepting the key concepts and truths taught in Theology of the Body. The enemy has used this heresy to prevent many from entering into the beautiful message given to us by Pope Saint John Paul II. Consequently, it had prevented me from entering into true healing that for me, because of my identity wounds with the Father, can ONLY come from affirmation. My distorted beliefs had convinced me to close myself off from affirmation, affection and from people. The truth is we all thrive when we are affirmed. Trauma results when we grow up without being affirmed as children.

It is one thing to know about Theology of the Body and it is quite another to be able to experience it. One of the major motivations of sharing my story in this book is to help uncover these lies from the enemy and to give readers courage through my example to walk into the wounds with Christ and ask Him to show you the wounds, show you the lies, show you the judgments you have made so you can renounce any inner vows and find true healing and restoration.

This healing experience was the catapult that would launch me into the craziest, most painful and spectacular events of my life and I thank God for it every day.

SEXUAL HEALING AND REDEMPTION

"He heals the brokenhearted and binds up their wounds." Psalm 147:3

When I arrived home after experiencing this very real taste of freedom and redemption, I saw my husband for perhaps the first time. My heart swelled with so much love that I felt it would overflow. He remarked that he noticed the changes in me and I sensed closeness between us that I had never experienced in the previous 15 years of marriage.

The next major transformation in my life came when I was pregnant with our 8th child. I was put on bed rest at about 7 months along. I had to stay in bed because of a separated pelvis. It was the loneliest time of my life; the suffering so was intense that there were days that I wished I would die. The pain was excruciating and through it all I expected my husband to say the things he had always said throughout the other pregnancies like "You're the one that wanted them." I felt I could not ask for him to comfort me or it would lead to another argument on NFP or about him wanting a vasectomy. But that is not what happened.

I was surprised at what transpired. Not only was he loving and affirming but also he truly seemed concerned for me and everyday he came home from work he would seek me out to spend time with me and love me. Every day I would be surprised that yet again he was loving and affirming and concerned with how I was doing. He always tried to think of me and make my life easier. Toward the end of the pregnancy my body had gotten so bad I could not walk nor could I sit upright. The pain continued and so did my despair. My doctor decided to have Jonah come early. To say I was relieved would be an understatement. I felt terrible for being unable to suffer through the last three weeks of pregnancy but I was so happy to see the finish line.

A few hours after inducing me I was holding Jonah Joseph Wylder King in my arms. I was never as relieved as I was that day to be able to sit upright and to walk to the bathroom without excruciating pain. I am constantly reminded how easy it is to take the simplest of things for granted.

When Jonah was only a few weeks old, I attended the "Sexual Healing and Redemption course" at the Theology of the Body Institute and my life would be forever changed. I am grateful now that my husband and I had grown closer during the time I was pregnant with Jonah. If we had not, I do not believe I could have handled what was coming.

It was the summer of 2009 when I attended the next course taught at the Theology of the Body Institute. Dr. Bob Schuchts of the Theology of the Body Healing and Training Center taught the course. The course was being offered at the Institute. At this point I was taking every new course offered because it was the only thing I had ever found that was making any kind of difference in myself and in my life. I felt unable to cope with trials without the retreats I would make there annually. I really believe that every person should take some kind of personal retreat at least once a year.

How are we capable of changing, growing or challenging ourselves to grow in holiness if we never take any time or effort to face painful places inside of us that we need to bring to God? Retreats are excellent ways to slowly peel back the layers in which we have stoned up our hearts of flesh so that we can love more rightly. We may not be able to prevent hurting our own children, but if we are constantly cleaning out our own hearts, we will be more capable of loving them and helping them to deal with their own hurts in life.

The weeklong retreat would have us reflecting on our own personal stories. We would be looking at our lives and discussing what kind of family, culture and faith life (if any) we had. We would look at our development and what it was like growing up focusing on the loss of innocence and when shame, sins, and wounds began. Finally, we would end the week discussing God's plan of redemption and how it was a plan of grace and restoration. It all sounded great right? Wrong.

It started out all right. In fact, God really prepared me for this day so well. I had with me a human shield. I often have used my babies to help me feel safe. I could hold Jonah in my arms and cuddle him, feeling his warm body against me. Jonah was a source of great comfort to me that week. Just having someone I could love that needed me and could not hurt me enabled me to bear the difficulties and painful work ahead of me. I believe God plans the circumstances that enable us to find healing and conversion. Just like a wedding planner, he goes over all the details and makes sure that everything is in place because he is gentle and desires for us to know and love him, not to torture or punish us. I was attending a teaching course and not a healing retreat so the process was more painful to me. I still believe it was worth all of the pain and suffering I went through.

As we began, we discussed God as love, creator, redeemer, father and bridegroom. A Quote from Kimberly Hahn, a mother and author of a book entitled *Life Giving Love*, in the booklet wrote, "Children are not possessions, the next thing to acquire after a car, a house, a dog. They are not a bonus earned but a gift freely given...Children do not have value because we give it to them. They have value for their own sake because God creates them in his image. Children are pure gift."

While I understood the reality of this being true, I had no understanding of it as an experience. I am not sure I have ever felt like a gift before. On the contrary, as I contemplated it, the feeling that came to me over and over again was that I was something to be endured, put up with, and suffered.

In fact, the thought that I was a gift was almost laughable. Anger began to rise up inside of me. I was so sick of all these 'goody two shoes' that write this tripe. They keep holding up an ideal and to me, it simply did not exist, making me feel even worse than I already did. I often get angry when I am presented with inconsistencies. It is another level of control. I need to be able to control it, even information to feel safe and protected.

To be given a truth that God loves everyone and sees us as gift made me mad because I never experienced this and the thought of it being true, but me not receiving it, exposed a lie I held, which was that I was unlovable, I was unworthy because I was bad. What I heard was children are good but not you because you are unworthy. It is funny how certain things can trigger us. When we begin to pay attention to what triggers us, we can begin to discover the lies. When we expose the lies, we can then bring Christ there to replace it with truth and we are then freed from the judgments we have made and the pain the lies inflict upon us.

I was unaware of any lies or judgments at this time in my healing. In fact, I felt the entire process was wounding me further. I began to feel rejected by everyone around me even when he or she was most probably as miserable as I was having his or her own wounds exposed. This reminds me of one of my favorite expressions: "You'd be surprised how little people think of you when you realize how little they did." This of course means most people are not thinking about you at all, except, of course, how it pertains to them. Most of us are thinking about ourselves.

The entire week I was there, anger continued to rise inside of me. I decided I needed to talk to the instructor. I had so many questions and they were burning in my chest and my eyes were doing everything they could to continue to blink back the hot tears that continued to manifest every time we discussed another area that touched on my wounds.

My entire life I have felt unworthy of anything. The situations of my childhood caused me to believe that my needs did not matter and that I must put the needs of others before myself. While this is an act of love and service, it is not something that we ask children to do, especially legitimate needs, so I carried with me scars and wounds from being treated as if my very legitimate needs were unimportant. That wound, was throbbing as the continued rejection reawakened the places inside that felt unseen and unheard.

When we came back as a group there was an announcement. We were all told that he would not take any more individual questions because he needed some time for himself. If we had questions we were to put them in a basket and he would try to answer them at the beginning of each class period. I waited for my question to be picked and it was not. The one time one of my questions was picked he did not answer it in the way meant and when I tried to raise my hand to ask him to clarify a point I was told there was no more time and no questions could be asked.

I was consumed with searing pain as if I had swallowed a hot lump of coal, yet every time I ventured into the hallway I was met with another student receiving a private session and sometimes by a student who had already had a chance to talk with him. The anger rose in me and became so toxic I began to think everyone around me were hypocrites and that no one really cared, even him. I was the selfish one, always selfish while other people continued to get their needs met and I did not. How is it I could be both selfish and ignored? I was in the pit of despair and felt that I was beginning to fall into a dark hole. Things got worse as we began to discuss child development, identity distortions, core wounds, and relational conflicts.

I learned that men deal with deep inadequacy wounds, fear of failure, being weak, and how they become dominating or passive as a result. In these words I saw my husband. I learned that women deal with a deep loneliness creating neediness in them or controlling issues. Women in this place begin to believe that she is undesirable and become fearful of being dominated or abandoned. In these words I saw myself.

I was seized with terror as I began to see my own identity issues, my own insecurities printed in black and white on the paper in front of me and there was nowhere to hide, not even behind my infant son asleep in my arms.

I thought doing the journaling questions at the end of the chapters would help me to resolve some of the painful questions in my mind, but they felt more like the protective scabs that covered my wounds were ripped off. I began to become aware of wounds I had forgotten, and wounds I was not even aware existed, became glaringly apparent. I was bleeding out emotionally. I felt as if someone had cut my wrists and the artery in my neck and the blood was pumping out with each beat of my heart. I felt as if I was lying in pools of my own blood I was abandoned into the abyss of my pain with no one noticing or even seeming to care.

My wounds of not having a voice and feeling unseen and unheard were stabbed into my soul even more deeply than they already were as the presenter walked away from me. Why did I come here? This was the first time I felt like coming to the Institute was a mistake. I was so desperate for love and affirmation and healing, yet it seemed like being desperate did nothing but make everything hurt more and feel more hopeless.

When we continued on in the course to the area on parental love and wounds I felt almost numb, as if the life inside me worth fighting for was drained out of me. I resolved myself to a place of knowing I was not worth anything and healing would elude me. It may sound like an exaggeration, but was in emotional pain as I dealt with the real traumas from my past childhood. The reason it was so painful was because I was going into the places of my heart and mind that had not yet been redeemed by the healing love of Jesus Christ. My heart at dark and ugly places that I was only able to go into with Jesus and Mary because if I had gone without their love and truth I would have been even more beaten up.

Perhaps the reason it became so intense was because there was a shift. I went from identifying myself in the wounds to seeing how I was now becoming the agent creating wounds in my own children. I felt powerless in this new knowledge and the pain of this realization was unbearable. It was like watching a baby stroller roll down a hill and running after it knowing there is just no way I could ever catch up before it goes off the cliff.

I learned how the tone of my voice could be damaging when I would be talking to my kids who were dealing with some of their own identity issues. What I was learning was opening my eyes as we discussed affection in ways I had not even thought of before. I had not considered that eye contact, and tone of voice as a way in which I could either affirm my children or wound them. I began to understand that the reason I had developed wounds of shame and rejection was because I had not been affirmed. These wounds became the roots of future addictions. Furthermore the lack of anything permanent in my life had caused insecurity and feelings of betrayal. We wound in the way we are wounded.

Learning all of this truth and knowledge without the healing or ability to know what or how to change anything in my life led me to despair. I understood ways I had wounded my children and was looking into the biggest of them all, my inability to give them affection. Affection has always been so difficult for me to give to my children. Babies were not a problem it was my children over the age of five. Once they were bigger, it felt more like an assault or like they were forcing something on me rather than something I was giving to them. I had never stopped to consider it other than to think something was wrong with me.

The guilt I had been carrying for so long came from judging myself for responding to my kid's needs of affection with anger or rejection. It has always been difficult to give affection to my kids. At times it was painful. It was so painful to me that at times I would even feel sick to my stomach and other times I would get angry and push them away saying, "Stop touching me!"

My guilt and shame was like a hot knife in my heart. I realized my tone of voice and my eye contact gave them the same message as my inability to give them affection. "I don't love you" was the message I was giving them and it was torture knowing that my wounds were making me powerless to change it.

It was bad enough that I felt like a bad mother now I realized how real the wounding was as I compared its affects on my own life. I was wounding my own children, but I had no way to change it, so what good was this stupid course doing me anyway?

As we began to learn about childhood traumas, a whole other can of worms opened. There are many traumas we experience as a child that we may never have realized are the source of what ails us. When I looked at a list of things that can cause wounds I realized that some of the things that I had not been given had caused as much damage if not more than what *had* been done to me. The following explanation of trauma is from James Friesen.

James Wilder et. Al,. The Life Model, 75

Type A Trauma's come from absence of good things we should all receive-things that give us emotional stability. These absences create difficulty in relationships...

1. Not being cherished and celebrated by one's parents

2. Not having experience of being a delight

3. Not having a parent take the time to understand who you are

4. Not receiving large amounts of non-sexual physical nurturing

5. Not receiving age appropriate limits

6. Not receiving adequate food, shelter clothing

7. Not being taught how to do things, to problem solve

8. Not given opportunities to develop personal resources and talents.

Type B Trauma is harmful by its presence....

1. Physical abuse, including face slapping, hair pulling

2. Any spanking that becomes violent

3. Sexual abuse including: inappropriate touching, sexual kissing, hugging, intercourse, oral or anal sex, voyeurism, exhibitionism, or the sharing of the parent's sexual experiences with the child.

4. Verbal abuses or name-calling

5. Abandonment by a parent

6. Torture or satanic ritual abuse

7. Witnessing someone else being abused

As for sexual abuse, there is overt (violation of innocence or sexual boundaries) and covert (emotional incest, implicit seduction). I had never known there were forms of sexual abuse that involved not actually having to touch someone and began to remember other events or people in my life that, under this new understanding, met the criteria of having more abusers in my life.

I began to spiral downward as I tried to make sense of all this new information and the more that I took in, more of my wounds were exposed. I was hurting deep down inside of me that I felt incapable of grasping what exactly it was hurting. I called my husband and he heard my grief, but when he asked me what was wrong I did not know what to say. What was wrong? I did not know except that it felt like grief.

No more! I could not endure it any longer. I could not remain in this dark place of suffering any longer. I was resolved that the instructor was going to talk to me, I needed him to help me. It became utterly unbearable to feel exposed, to be so aware of my failures, of my deep hurts and emptiness inside. I no longer cared about the teachers need to use the restroom, sleep or eat, I was going to talk to him or leave on the next flight out.

I approached the instructor and asked him to speak to me. I stood there shaking as I spoke in a high staccato voice. My whole body seemed to jerk as I tried to speak doing all I could to keep what little control I had so that I would not crumple to the floor in front of him.

The tears welled up hot and fast into my eyes and burst out like a flood down my face drenching my shirt. The words were more like sobs and I am not even sure how much he could even understand as the days of rejection and torture poured out of me. I told him, through my tears and sobbing, that I needed his help.

His eyes opened wide and I waited for his response. He looked honestly and sincerely concerned for me. He took me by the arm into a private room. I did not even care anymore at this point as to what I looked like or sounded like. The floodgates had been opened and the emotional gush of pain and anguish poured out of me for him to deal with. I did not even care if anyone was around or heard me. Just to allow it to come out was already bringing me a small sense of relief. Angry emotional outbursts were the only way I had ever coped with the pain in my life, grieving was not yet I I know it is a necessary part of being able to begin healing. We need to be able express our pain and to have it be heard.

He sat me down on the couch and began to speak gently to me. He asked if he could go through the healing model with me that we had been discussing during the week. That, of course, was all I had wanted.

I nodded my head and blew my nose. He asked me what was causing the most pain. I shared with him I had been abused. He was telling us to go God our Father for our Identity and Jesus for healing but I could not go to Jesus for healing because I felt He abandoned me. I could not go to God the Father because He allowed these things to happen.

He began by praying to the Holy Spirit asking Him to lead me to the memory or event in which I first believed that I was abandoned or could not go to God. I was led to the room where I was abused when I was 3 years old. He asked me to picture it as if I was there as a child once again. He asked me about how I felt, what I was thinking and what was happening. Then he asked me a profound question: "Where is Jesus?" At first I thought he was being obtuse. "What do you mean where is Jesus? He is not here!" I said in a surprised tone. I wondered, how sick is this guy to think Jesus is there in the room while I am being violated?

I cannot remember if he asked me to picture Jesus in the room or if Jesus just appeared in the memory, but all of a sudden I saw Jesus by the door and he was weeping. I became aware of Jesus weeping for the loss of my innocence. He was weeping that this man was so willing to participate in hurting me and he was weeping at the evil and sin that was in that room with me, his precious child. I felt the preciousness of being his little one. This experience of Jesus in the room with me at the moment of the abuse instantly created a huge change inside of me. The only way I can describe it is to say that my entire life up to this point, I had been praying to Jesus who was up in heaven with His Father. Now, I realized that Jesus was here with me in every moment of my life. In that moment, he was not only here with me but he was weeping the same intense grief that I had within me at that very moment.

Dr. Bob asked me several questions leading me to the lies and judgments that were causing so much pain for me all week. When I would encounter confusion or some kind of block, he would pray out loud to Jesus and the Holy Spirit to remove the barrier or to "show Christina." I did not know what to expect, but he told me to pay attention to pictures or memories. He told me to trust the process and just be still and describe anything I noticed.

The Holy Spirit knows all of the secret places of our heart and knows how to communicate to us what we have forgotten or what we need to look at and how to look at it. To ask the Holy Spirit to help in the process of inner healing makes sense. What took place through this process can only be described as a miracle.

After a few minutes of this, he helped me uncover one of the vows I had made in creating a fortress around my heart. The fortress kept out those who could hurt me and so it served a purpose of sorts (so I thought) but the walls that keep out the bad guy also kept out God. The vows we make are of our own freewill and God never violates our freedoms so we must be willing to suffer that thing, we must be willing to go into those bad memories or circumstances to discover the lie so we can open up the door for healing.

I felt so much love and peace inside of my heart that I had never experienced before. It permeated my very being. The sense of relief was so immediate that I almost could not remember what had seemed so troubling to me that whole week.

I once heard a speaker say that our bad memories or experiences are like a bad neighborhood, you don't want to go in their alone or you will get the you-know-what kicked out of you. This is very true. The enemy always accuses us and Jesus always invites. If the words whispered in your ear sound like being accused, then you know whom that is: the evil one. Jesus is so gentle and loving, he only invites and he never goes faster than you are able or willing to go. If the enemy tries to remind you of how unworthy or flawed you are, tell him, "God knew what He was getting when He made me. I am no surprise to God. If you don't like that, take it up with the Creator." We must always go with Jesus and Mary, especially if we had mothers or fathers who rejected or abandoned us. We may not fully understand or even believe it, but God loves us with an unfathomable love. We are very good.

That week I was being beaten up emotionally until I entered into the love of Christ. Without it, I was left to see only my ugliness and the ugliness of others without compassion or mercy. Once I received the love of Christ, I could look at the ugliness of my own sinful actions without being consumed by despair.

Dr. Bob continued to ask questions and pray through it all so that I could identify the lies. Once I was able to identify the lie causing me the greatest distress and from where it originated, he asked me to say the belief out loud and renounce it in the name of Jesus Christ. The power of Jesus Christ to heal and restore me as a new creation was and still is very real. I had no idea that all I had to do was to ask and receive.

As I said it out loud, tears poured out of me as well as a painful grief I was unaware was in me. It was a deep pain from so many years of judgment and it was being emptied out. To hear it spoken aloud made the pain that much more acute. It was like taking wire bristles and scrubbing at an infected sore. He then asked me to renounce the vows I had made to myself in an attempt to protect myself. "In the name of Jesus Christ of Nazareth who comes in flesh, I renounce the lie that I am unlovable and that the abuse was my fault." As I renounced the lie he smiled and asked me to say it again. I felt a shift. He asked me to renounce it again. Just like that, I felt a freedom as if someone had opened the door to a hot room and a summer breeze washed into the room gently stirring the curtains and making a sleeping cat ears pick up. The washing was of my heart and it refreshed my soul.

I asked him what had just happened.. He smiled and chuckled as he asked me to say the lie I had believed once more. I hesitated at first but then said it. When I said the lie, I began to laugh and he asked me why I was laughing. "Because that is not true!" I said with such joy and relief that I thought I had just witnessed a miracle and, in fact, I believe I had.

In all of the years of therapy, counseling, and Psychiatrists, I had never experienced anything close to what happened in the space of less than five minutes. In a word: freedom. I experienced a freedom like I have never known before. The pain, the torture, and the grief from the week were not present in that moment. I felt more fully alive, as if I had just lost 100 pounds.

I realized at the end of that retreat I needed more of that. At home, I told my husband all that transpired. I told him about another retreat coming up that would deal with healing the "Whole Person" and I felt that I had to go. I am not sure what I did or said to convince him, but he supported me and we found a way to afford the airfare to send me.

I had never attended two retreats in the span of thirty days, but I turned right around and went to Florida for a three day healing retreat taught by Dr. Bob Schuchts and his staff. Once again I experienced something on an even deeper level, I felt redemption. I felt redeemed in Jesus Christ, I was purchased at a price and my value was beyond compare. It is important that we realize there is an enemy out there prowling about seeking the ruin of souls and it is not just our negative self talk and the "limitations" we place on ourselves doing all of this emotional damage. There is a real enemy that has been the Father of lies since the very beginning and we are at war. In fact, he understands our sexuality and the great mystery better than us. He uses that knowledge to create the very wounds from which to enter, and then oppress us, severing us from the creator and making us lose hope and ultimately our souls.

TARGETED BY THE DEVIL
SPRITUAL WARFARE

"For our wrestling is not against flesh and blood; but against principalities and power, against the rulers of the world of this darkness, against the spirits of wickedness in the high places."
Ephesians 6:12

St. Michael the Arc Angel, defend us in battle. Be our protection against the wickedness and snares of the devil. May God rebuke him, we humbly pray, and do thou, O Prince of the heavenly hosts, by the power of God, thrust into hell Satan, and all the evil spirits, who prowl about the world seeking the ruin of souls. Amen.

Are there demons "prowling about the world seeking the ruin of souls"? Yes. The devil does exist and we are in a battle for souls: your soul and mine. If you want to know the thing that is most valued and held in high honor by God, look to what the evil one attacks and profanes: the body, our sexuality, love, unborn babies, and children.

All abuse is wrong and effects us in what can be profoundly deep wounds, yet sexual abuse is distinct. It wounds at a place in which our identity in God comes from. It creates a split within the very self. It is intimate, it is penetrative, and its effects can be felt through the generations.

Abuse, neglect, and trauma are a reality of sin in our world from broken and wounded people hurting others in the way they were wounded. But there is even more to it than that. It is a powerful way for the evil one to target persons that he identifies as dangerous to his own mission. That's right! It is not random. It was not bad luck that four separate people sexually abused me. It was because I was targeted. But how and why is this possible? First, we must understand the evil in which we are dealing with.

Fr. Robert Altier is a priest whom I was referred to by the Vicar General of my Diocese. He has helped me understand how there are specific spirits that not only enter in through wounds, but also need the wounds in order to infest or oppress someone. He writes for the website www.Courageous Priests.com

He described one kind of spirit as "ministering spirits." They are a higher order of angel and he writes that "...they are the ones that live within the wounds that are inflicted upon us from the time that we are quite young, when there are traumatic things that happen in our lives when we are young (before 12 years-old)."

He says that these spirits wrap around our personality and so they are very difficult to get rid of. He goes on to say:

"The problem with ministering spirits is, first of all, they are exceedingly intelligent, which is why they go after little children rather than adults because their arrogance will not allow them to do anything else. They try to hide behind the personality of the people. These are the ones that will cause pride, selfishness, anger, and also fear. So when we see these kinds of problems in our lives, these are things that are rooted deep, deep within ourselves. They are in the wounds that were inflicted when we were young, and the only way to be able to get rid of them is to get inside and be able to address the woundedness, to heal those wounds that are there through forgiveness, through working through the various things in prayer. Slowly, we will be able to push these things away." http://www.courageouspriest.com/father-robert-altier-reality-action-demons

Satan understands better than we do the relationship of physical and spiritual, as well as how being created male and female is meant to be an icon revealing the love of the Trinity, our call to union, communion with one another, and ultimately with God.

This is perhaps why the devil hates us so much: that God would take the dirt of the earth and unite His spirit to it and call it His own image. The fact that angels are to serve this dirt of the earth must be what Satan's pride could not accept. Because he was pure spirit and had full knowledge of what he would be rejecting, his fall was permanent and irrevocable.

Sexual abuse, in light of this understanding of the union of the body and soul, is not just an abuse experienced by the body, but it is an abuse of our very person. Its effects create barriers to our ability to be in relationship with one another and with God.

What do I mean by personhood? Pope Saint John Paul II wrote in *Evangelium Vitae* that the union of the physical and spiritual, in other words, the body and soul is "person."

If we had spiritual eyes to see (and some saints and mystics did see into the spiritual realm) we would be able to see which persons were baptized and which were not, which persons were in a state of grace and those that were in a state of mortal sin. The body makes visible the invisible says Pope Saint John Paul II because there is a union of spirit and matter because there is a spiritual reality we cannot see. Each and every one of us is seen by the enemy, as well as by the angels created by God, in the spiritual realm.

St. Faustina and a number of other saints talk about how the enemy seems to target those who have a call to priesthood and sainthood. While we are all called to be saints, there are certain souls that are called to build up Christ's church in a larger way than most and it is as if the enemy has learned to identify which souls are most dangerous to him.

The Devil cannot know God's plan, but he has learned to see which souls have a mystical receptivity to the divine. Saints have said that warrior angels are given to persons with these missions or other angels to protect them and their call by God to fulfill it. Perhaps it is in this way the enemy has learned to identity which persons are dangerous to him. Whatever it is, I was healed in a profound way when I realized that God did not abandon me or fail to protect me. In fact the evil one targeted me as he somehow could see that God had anointed me with a call to evangelize on a global scale. I was dangerous to the devil. He had to try and take me out, to cripple me and sexual abuse was his weapon.

In my travels and speaking, I have met many people who are writers, speakers, authors, teachers, and even priests who have been sexually abused. All of these people are in public ministry that brings Christ to the world. Is it a coincidence that they were sexually abused? I think not. Now we know. If you were sexually abused, I pray this truth brings freedom from the lie that God abandoned you. The real truth that has been hidden from you was that the enemy targeted you, not because you are bad but because you are very, very good.

The devil first targets us with abortion and if that does not work he targets us with sexual abuse. Why is sexual abuse so different than physical or emotional abuse? It is because of the deep union of the body and soul. Our personhood is tied to being created in God's image and likeness made as male and female. Our sexuality reveals the mystery of union of physical and spiritual as well as being the image of God and the call to union and communion revealed in the trinity.

To abuse us here, in this sacred place, creates an effect that is so intimate; our very person is fractured, as well as our relationship to our Creator. Abortion and sexual abuse are weapons used by the evil one dangerous people he identifies as dangerous to him.

I was sexually abused because I live in a sinful world and there are many people that are infected by their wounds. They wound in the way they were wounded. The enemy sees those who are a danger to him. He sees those that God has called into existence for the building up of Christ's Church and like a General at war, he targets them so as to remove them from the battle ground through abortion or to disable them through sexual abuse.

As a person who suffered from sexual abuse, it has been comforting and very healing for me to know that God did not abandon me; rather the evil one targeted me. This is war. We are at war. It really is not about me at all, but rather it is about the enemy and God. The enemy hates God and seeks his revenge by hurting and wounding the most innocent - children. This gives the enemy satisfaction because it causes God the most suffering.

The enemy knows that God has created the sexual union to have a spiritual effect upon persons. The evil one uses this truth for evil purposes knowing that God will not change the "truth" because this a contradiction. If the truth is that the sexual union of man and woman in the marital embrace is a conduit of sanctifying grace, then the enemy realizes that persons engaging in the same activity under the most blasphemous of circumstances, like rape or abuse, could then become a conduit of evil. The good news is that Christ came to set the captives free and that freedom is called Deliverance.

DELIVERANCE

"The spirit of the Lord is upon me, because He anointed me to preach the gospel to the poor. He has sent me to proclaim deliverance to the captives and recovery of sight to the blind, to set free those who are oppressed..." Luke 4:18

Fr. Robert Altier of Courageous Priests explained it to me like this:

"The devil is a great legalist but God is not. The devil uses the rules to create evil effect; it is his only way to have any real power. The truth is the devil has no power at all. He merely uses the power of God and manipulates the rules to cause the perverse effects and he needs the free participation (freewill) of people to physicalize it."

God desires to be in covenant with us. Covenants are about being in an intimate relationship with God. The devil can only create contracts, which are about keeping us from being in relationship with God.

It is as if the devil is shouting out, "I have a contract! I have every right to be here!" This is why deliverance is very important to inner healing. While inner healing is about healing our emotions and healing our relationship with God, deliverance is about freeing us from the contracts we have entered into with the devil. Sometimes we must be delivered so we can remove the barriers that are preventing us from being healed.

A person can go to Mass, pray more, do a novena, a pilgrimage. While all of these things can help, if the evil one has a contract, he is not going anywhere. Deliverance is how we nullify the contracts and legal grounds from which the enemy uses to infest, oppress, or possess us.

Deliverance is the expelling of demons through the power of Jesus Christ. There are many levels of deliverance. Simple deliverance can and should be done by anyone and everyone who has been baptized in the name of the Father, and of The Son, and of The Holy Spirit. Exorcism is different. It is for priestly authority only because it directly deals with the devil, while simple deliverance is about helping a person exercise (no pun intended) their freewill so as to renounce and break agreements with the evil one. If a person is unable to help themselves an exorcist (who has been trained and is under obedience and protection of the Church) is needed to help the person in their fight against the evil one.

"All Christians potentially possess the special Charism needed to expel demons by virtue of their baptism. This, at any rate, was the case until the third or fourth centuries when an order of exorcists began to emerge in some part of the Church. () Whereas before, the work of the exorcist was seen as a universal gift granted to all believers by God, now it was becoming an appointment by the Church. What was once a function rapidly became a title and an office." Fr. Jeffrey S. Grob

Deliverance is scary to some people. They see movies like *The Exorcist* or *The Rite* and they think deliverance is about warfare with Satan. Deliverance is more about asking forgiveness for our sins, breaking our agreements with the evil one, and reconciling ourselves with God using the power of Jesus Christ to do it.

While praying for inner healing is prayer directed toward God, deliverance is recognizing who is responsible for attacking us and commanding him to leave. It is directed at the enemy in that we are renouncing our vows to him and breaking our union with him all in the name of Jesus Christ. (More in the chapter on "Becoming Unbound")

God always takes evil and brings a better good out of it. The very wounds inflicted upon me have become the very places that have helped me to love more perfectly. "With His stripes we are healed." Isaiah 53:5 This has been very healing for me to contemplate. Confession is a powerful part of deliverance ministry. Taking our hurts and wounds into confession and asking God to forgive us for hating the people who hurt us rather than hating the devil, is a great place to start breaking contracts. Forgiving a person who hurt us does not mean what they did was not wrong. After all, it was their own free-will that allowed the devil to work through them. However, when we see who our true enemy is, we can then realize that those who hurt us are under a terrible oppression and in need of deliverance themselves.

The renewing of our baptismal vows is a powerful form of deliverance because it breaks our agreements with the evil one and it restores our agreements to follow Christ. If you can do this to a person that is in an official position of the Church it is even more powerful (priest or deacon) but you can do this yourself as well as your freewill is what allowed the evil one permission to oppress you and your freewill can renounce that permission.

V. Do you reject Satan?

R. I do.

V. And all his works?

R. I do.

V. And all his empty promises?

R. I do.

V. Do you believe in God, the Father Almighty, creator of heaven and earth?

R. I do.

V. Do you believe in Jesus Christ, his only Son, our Lord, who was born of the Virgin Mary was crucified, died, and was buried, rose from the dead, and is now seated at the right hand of the Father?

R. I do. V. Do you believe in the Holy Spirit, the holy Catholic church, the communion of saints, the forgiveness of sins, the resurrection of the body, and life everlasting?

R. I do.

V. God, the all-powerful Father of our Lord Jesus Christ has given us a new birth by water and the Holy Spirit, and forgiven all our sins. May he also keep us faithful to our Lord Jesus Christ forever and ever.

R. Amen.

Deliverance ministry and Inner Healing is the utilization of prayer and spiritual direction or counseling to help someone uncover where the agreements with the enemy have been made. It then helps us to use the authority of Jesus Christ that we have by virtue of our baptism to break free from any oppression that coming into agreement with the Father of Lies has afflicted on us.

Call upon the legion of angels that God has given us to do spiritual battle. We have might weapons in this battle for souls and it is about time we used them. St. Michael leads the charge and he is a mighty warrior. But you must ask to receive. Angels have free-will too, so if you want them to intercede, you must ask them. Ask your guardian angel to help you. Pray to your guardian angel and St. Michael every day, confess your sins, renew your baptismal promises and you will see the oppression lift. I guarantee it. You will begin to experience freedom.

When we learn to separate out the sin from the sinner we can forgive the person knowing that they were created for greatness, they are children of God, they are people falling under the weight of their weakness, and devoid of the necessary graces to perfect their nature.

God makes all things new and He has given me a platform to bring truth, life, and love to others that have been targeted. Christ has come to set the captives free. You are being called to reclaim your own greatness. Ask God to help you see with new eyes. You may not be able to forgive, but Jesus can. Let your prayer be: "Jesus, I cannot do this but you can. Help me to forgive. Give me your heart."

BE NOT AFRAID

"I plead with you--never, ever give up on hope, never doubt, never tire, and never become discouraged. Be not afraid." Saint John Paul II

I remember as a kid falling off of my bike and scraping my knees up so bad that they were filled with gravel and blood. Imagine if we just covered them up with a Band-Aid instead of cleaning them out or treating them with antibiotic ointment? It would be an infected mess of pus and the bandage would dry into the cut. After enough time, the infection would spread into our blood and make our whole body sick. It is no different with emotional or spiritual wounds. If they are left untreated, they poison our entire system.

I was so afraid of the pain required to rip off the bandage, as well as what I would find when I did, that I had lived with the wounds and allowed the infection to spread. The sexual abuse I suffered had presented a lie that being vulnerable means being violated. Because I was not yet aware of this lie, I believed it was truth. I was living out the lie and was controlling, overbearing, and bossy. I would think many women believe vulnerability is weakness, especially if they were abused.

As I attempted to run away from my pain I would use whatever means necessary to feel comfortable. I convinced myself that control was how I would do it. Rather than suffer through the difficulties and painfulness I attempted to control people and circumstances in my life to feel more confortable in my own skin. What I had not yet learned was that I was not made for comfort, I was made for greatness.

"The World offers you comfort. But you were not made for comfort. You were made for greatness!" Pope Benedict XVI

The only mother and father I had known had rejected, neglected, and abandoned me in so many ways that I found it difficult to trust God. Fathers are to be a sign to children that God is loving and protective.

Father's are supposed to be dependable. Mothers teach children to trust and put faith and hearts into relationships, especially with God. If parents fail to give children this truth by example, then mother wounds and father wounds develop and these wounds may prevent the children from entering into the "deep". Consequently, God's desire for His children is not understood.

"Do not be afraid. Do not be satisfied with mediocrity. Put out into the deep and let down your nets for a catch." Saint John Paul II

Mother and father wounds affect our identity as persons. My identity was based on my beliefs rather than who I truly was. Instead of going to God and asking, "Who do you say that I am?" my mistrust of God led me to other people to shape my identity.

The identity I had in my family was that I was a manipulative child, that used my sexuality to get attention, and instigated the circumstances, which led to me being abused in, at least one, if not more circumstances. Perhaps for some people it is easier to label a child or blame them than to look to their own actions (or lack of action) to prevent or even discover the abuse in the first place. Perhaps it is someone's own brokenness or wounded heart that prevents them from seeing what is obvious to others.

Whatever the reason, the effects of abuse went unnoticed to those around me. It did not change the fact that I felt unheard, without a voice, and somehow bad and unworthy of being protected. This is how the enemy works. He distorts the truth and turns it into a lie that causes so much pain that people turn inward and find ways to protect them. Instead of turning to God, they turn to false gods, idols if you will, to help manage the pain or cope with circumstances. My identity was distorted by a lie. I believed no one cared which meant I was not worthy of protection or possibly didn't deserve it. In an attempt to hold onto my value, I made my "god" myself. I gave myself value.

I would try to prove my value with my looks or my intelligence. The sin of pride grew in me because I was making myself the source of my own identity. Anger would well up when someone would not affirm me, so control became my other new god. I would find ways to manipulate others so they will like me, all in an attempt to hold onto a tiny and fragile image of the "self" I was trying to protect. When they still did not like me, I would despair. I would become slothful, making television my new god. I would sit for hours watching television to numb my pain.

When we turn to something other than God, we chose a false god. This is the breaking of the first commandment, which says we will not worship a false god. When we are in pain, the enemy comes to us and proposes to us. If we accept his proposal, we accept his lie and a new belief is formed in our minds. When we act upon the belief, we are worshiping with our very lives this false god and the vows we make become the very chains that keep us in bondage.

When events in our lives cause us suffering, the devil, the enemy of our soul, comes to us in that moment and proposes a lie to us much like a groom would propose marriage. If we believe the lie he proposes, we are then opening ourselves to him. This is a foothold. St. Paul tells us how sin can becomes a foothold using anger as an example.

"Do not be angry and sin in your anger and give the devil a foothold". (Eph 4:26-27)

We are either in relationship with God or relationship with the devil. We are either walking in truth or walking in a lie. When Eve was in the Garden of Eden, the devil came and proposed his lie to her that God could not be trusted, that he was keeping something back from her by not allowing her to eat from the Tree of Knowledge. He was proposing that God did not love her. When Eve ate the apple, she accepted the proposal of the devil, she accepted his lie, and just like any marriage, there was fruit that came from her accepting the proposal. The fruit was death. When we accept the lies the devil proposes, we our severing our union with God and are uniting ourselves to the evil one.

With our freewill, we are choosing to be in relationship with the liar and this foothold we have given him will grow like a cancer if we ignore it. Like cancer spreads in our bodies, so does the affects of the lies we consent to believe. These footholds turn into strongholds.

"A stronghold is any pattern of behavior in your life that you know is against the will of God but continues to persist even when you try to change it." (Healing The Whole Person Dr Bob Schuchts Anatomy of a wound).

This pattern is a result of the barriers we have built around our heart, brick-by-brick, lie-by-lie, and vow-by-vow in an attempt to protect ourselves from being hurt or suffering. The problem with putting up walls around our heart is that we keep out the good along with the bad. We become like a prisoner within a castle and the stronghold keeps us there. It makes us feel sick and we know we are not at peace.

"We all have a sense of what it would look like for us to be spiritually free. We expect that we would be at peace, untroubled by fears, stress or anxiety. If we were truly free, we would not get a sick feeling in our stomach when we thought about enduring a family Thanksgiving dinner; the mean words Aunt Maude spoke over us when we were six would no longer rankle. If we were free, we would have a solid core of joy inside, rather than a heavy weight that seems always present in our midsections." (Resisting The Devil, Neal Lozano, pg. 11)

For years I had tried counseling. It brought some temporary relief, taught me some coping skills, and gave me a means by which to deal with the distress symptoms that resulted from believing the lies. Counseling did nothing to change the strongholds in my life, nor did it help me bring them down.

Praying was helpful and was definitely a step in the right direction, as God is the one who can help expose the lies so we know where to start. However, unless I used the weapons spoken of by St. Paul, I would only be managing my pain rather than finding true freedom and healing.

I had tried medication, which afforded some relief. Perhaps it helped me manage my anxiety that was related to the stronghold, but a chemical does not cause strongholds, so freedom eluded me. A stronghold is an action of our freewill and unless we take it down with our own freewill it will not be removed by medication.

For years I have lived with the guilt that I was such a bad child that I either deserved the abuse or that I somehow instigated it. I have been told my entire life that no one liked me, I was a loud and outspoken child, and relatives and friends did not like me coming over. I was told I was selfish and manipulative. I have been reminded that I was not planned or even wanted. I have been told that I came out of the womb screaming, insinuating that I have been causing trouble since the day I was born. Perhaps it was meant to be a funny story, but the message I heard was that I was bad. I have lived with so much shame. I still struggle with it and must go to God the Father for my identity, which is difficult when you have trust issues and father wounds.

How did I cope with such deep identity wounds? I made my exterior my identity; my sexuality was what seemed to get my needs met so it seemed logical to continue allowing others to use me. I believed that love was use.

Some women use their sexuality to control or dominate men, and others reject their femininity, embracing masculinity, which they believe to be more powerful. After all, we all need affection, affirmation, care, concern, love, connection, and relationship. We are all so willing to accept the counterfeit rather than what our hearts truly long for, and I was no different. I became an object and found ways to be used.

Some see femininity as a weakness, or worse yet sinful, and seek to cover it up, play it down, hide it under a metaphorical bushel basket. I did two out of three.

I definitely saw femininity as weak so I went the other direction. I decided to use my femininity as power. A more modern term could be understood as feminism. Authentic femininity is very good and a beautiful thing, helping to reveal the call to union and communion.

Femininity has now been replaced in the world with feminism, which is nothing, like authentic femininity. Feminism seeks to remove the differences between men and women and, in fact, to make women more like men. It emasculates me, it is sterile like barren wombs, and it rejects the different complementarities of our sexuality.

Many women use sex as a weapon. I was one of these women. I used my femininity to control or manipulate others. What I did not realize is that this ends up emasculating men, burning a lot of bridges, and earned me my own terrible nicknames. Being this kind of woman made me feel powerful. I was like a steamroller. I was proud that I did not know the meaning of the world *can't*. If I wanted to do something, I did it.

Vulnerability was my enemy. It is still my nemesis, but I am on the road to recovery and I am beginning to see it as courage and living through my heart rather than just my head filled with mistruths.

I am not going to tell you that healing isn't painful, when in fact, it is excruciating. However, the pain of living with wounds is beyond excruciating. Why did I turn to false idols and begin to make gods out of all of those things? Because I thought they would give some satisfaction or some escape from the pain of my wounds. If we sin in our wounds we end up helping the enemy build up a stronghold around us preventing healing to take place. So how was I going to break free from the strongholds? I would have to be willing to suffer.

"Therefore, since the Messiah suffered in a mortal body, you, too, must arm yourselves with the same determination, because the person who has suffered in a mortal body is done with sin..." 1 Peter 4:1 NIV Bible

When we are willing to suffer the original thing we were running away from, turn back to God, and ask him to help us, then and only then do we acquire the actual graces to practice the virtues necessary in overcoming a particular sin in our life. It is only the contrary virtue that enables us to overcome areas of sinfulness in our lives. We overcome Pride with Humility, Greed with Charity, Lust with Chastity, Gluttony with Temperance, Sloth with Diligence, Anger with Forgiveness, Envy with Kindness.

The abuse, trauma, and neglect I experienced created a feeling of powerlessness and so I turned to my god-of-control in an attempt to control everything and everyone. Most likely it also resulted in distrust, fear, and un-forgiveness and myriad of other dysfunction in my life.

The difference is, once healing begins the pain is transformed and becomes joy whereas staying wounded remains excruciating and, in some people, can even bring about disease and even mental illness. When we forgive people who have hurt us, we then begin to embody the merciful heart of Jesus Christ. Anger cannot remain where one has softened their hearts and become forgiving and merciful. Anger cannot abide where a heart has turned to God and begins to relinquish its power in exchange for his grace and his will in their life.

I see its effects today in members of my own family. They refuse to press into the pain of guilt they have for allowing my abuse and neglect. Instead of facing the guilt and asking God to forgive them, they blame me and minimize how bad it really was. They tell me I have made things up, they tell me to ignore or forget what happened to me, or they just get angry and yell about how hard it was for them. All of this is a way of avoiding the pain of dealing with the truth. The irony is, we are all in pain anyway. We think by minimizing, denying or blaming others that we are avoiding the pain and suffering of the circumstances that haunt us. The reality is, we suffer it worse because we remain alone in our miserable prison experiencing tastes of hell on earth.

We put ourselves on the cross and are crucified to it rather than allowing a loving savior to help us bear the weight of the burden and struggle. This is freewill. We all can choose what we will do with our pain. I, for one, have found facing it and pressing into the wounds brings a great relief and freedom that has transformed my life.

How does one begin to gain the courage to peel off the temporary bandage we use to hide our wounds so that we can actually expose it? The first thing that I had to do was to become vulnerable. To be vulnerable, we must not be afraid to look at the wounds and to expose them. Then, we must go into the wounds. It's like the story of St. Thomas in the bible. We know him as Doubting Thomas. Thomas doubted that Jesus had rose from the dead and was standing before him in the upper room. To help Thomas believe, Jesus had Thomas put his fingers into his pierced side. This is a beautiful reminder that Jesus

Christ overcame death and when He was resurrected, His wounds were still there, but they were redeemed.

Why were His hands and feet still pierced? Because He wanted us to see how powerful redemption is and how our wounds, once redeemed become a visible sign to the world of His power. This is what I had to grasp for myself. The truth that my wounds, once redeemed would inspire others to believe in the glory of God and His ability to overcome every evil.

Could it be that regardless of what I have ever done that God still has always desired for me to exist? I believe that it is and that He has chosen each of us for some great purpose. I am proof that we should not be afraid to expose our own wounds to the great physician who is our Living God. I am living proof that He will not abandon you there but he also will not trample on your freewill. Each of us must be the one to open the door; only you can be the one to invite Him in.

He is a gentle lover of our souls and He will not open the gate before you are ready. He moves slowly and in your time. Another irony is that there may come a time when you want to rush forward and He will hold you back. He knows what you can handle and will not overwhelm you or lead you into despair. The words "Jesus I trust in you" begin with being vulnerable enough to be seen. To remove the metaphorical fig leaf and let God see you and let yourself be truly seen by Him. He can take all of it, even your anger. Hold nothing back from Him. He wants it all. He wants you and all that comes with you, even what needs to be healed.

So how did I come to learn all of this? It would be over the course of my marriage. My husband and I met in college and got married two months after he graduated. The first thing we did was getting married and the second thing was to move away from the people who were not a good influence on us. We moved back to my husband's hometown to begin our married life together. Neither of us was really practicing the faith at this point so we were married in a courthouse by a justice of the peace. We had our reception at the restaurant where I worked. The next few years were like a carnival ride as I began to change interiorly. I hungered for more knowledge about the Blessed Mother and my

Catholic faith.

I began to see my faith as something beautiful. I also began to feel ashamed of my own selfishness and weakness of faith. I did not feel accused in this, but rather realized I had missed out on something willingly because of my sin and was ashamed because of the love growing inside of me that I did not love Christ as much as He showed me He loved me.

I began reading books by the dozen. I attended lectures on the faith. I started praying the Rosary. This began giving me tremendous insight. I went back to confession for the first time in years and let all the horrible sins spill out. I felt so free and refreshed having experienced a renewed gift from my childhood. This was just another God-moment in a line of many more to come over the next few years and, boy, was I going to need them!

I had some really big things to deal with if I was going to keep my marriage together and grow in my newfound faith. Religion became another expression of my idol, which was of course just another means of control.

Healing is like an onion. Just as an onion has layers so too does healing. What I have learned is that even though God can just heal us in an instant, it is often a mercy that He heals us in layers. To force us to deal with our sins before we are able to handle all of the shame that goes with it. To do so would be like kicking in our doors and throwing us into the sewage of our lives. He is a gentle loving savior and He will go as slowly as necessary to help us find true and lasting freedom.

I certainly began to find some freedom when I found God because He is the source of healing. The problems came when the old wounds surfaced. Because I had not recognized the lies and beliefs in my heart and had not renounced the vows and false gods, I continued very slowly, stumbling along the way.

I believe many people fall under a spirit of false religion or legalism. It is another attempt of the evil one to present a lie and corrupt the source of healing. From the beginning he has lied to us about who God is and has tried to get us to believe that God cannot be trusted. For others, the devil convinces them they must work their salvation out. They must do this or that. They must embody holiness like a cloak to be seen and applauded by other holy people.

My journey of healing took a slight detour when I decided to fix myself. That was my first mistake. I cannot fix anyone much less myself. However, I had not yet learned this lesson, so I decided the best way to "fix" my life was to become holy. What would transpire would be greater woundedness, as well as driving a wedge between my family and I. My extended family would call me a religious fanatic and most probably anyone else that met me would have agreed. I might have removed the bandage, but instead of cleaning out the wounds, I was just covered them up again with a fancier looking Band-Aid.

BECOMING UNBOUND

"Put on the whole armor of God, so that you may be able to stand against the wiles of the devil. For our struggle is not against enemies of blood and flesh, but against the rulers, against the authorities, against the cosmic powers of this present darkness, against the spiritual forces of evil in the heavenly places. Therefore take up the whole armor of God, so that you may be able to withstand on that evil day, and having done everything, to stand firm. Stand therefore, and fasten the belt of truth around your waist, and put on the breastplate of righteousness. As shoes for your feet put on whatever will make you ready to proclaim the gospel of peace. With all of these] take the shield of faith, with which you will be able to quench all the flaming arrows of the evil one. Take the helmet of salvation, and the sword of the Spirit, which is the word of God." Eph 6:10-18

Once I realized I was bound up and need to be delivered what did I do next? I began buying books on deliverance. The word deliverance can scare some people but I like what Neal Lozano say's about it in his book "Resisting the Devil." He says; "To say that deliverance is about the devil is like saying that the Exodus story in Genesis is about Pharaoh." Deliverance is about Christ setting the captives free. It is about the power of Jesus Christ that is given to us in baptism, renewed and refreshed through repentance and reconciliation and empowered by the gifts of the Holy Spirit released in confirmation. However, some of us have not been renewed and refreshed for a long time. Some of us have not been reconciled at all nor have we asked for the Holy Spirit to release the gifts of our confirmation. We must be courageous and ask for double portion like Elijah did in the bible.

When we are not free to love and be loved then we are not making the invisible visible through our lives and our example. We are to be the body of Christ, yet some of us are still bound up from the lies we believe, the vows we have made, the judgments of others and when this effects our identities we are cut off from the very life giving source that we must draw upon. So how do we listen to the Holy Spirit? How do we find freedom? How do we refresh, reconcile and release the Holy Spirit in us and through us? The first thing we have to do is pray to the Holy Spirit.

COME HOLY SPIRIT COME!

It can begin with simplest of prayers, really it can. One of the books I came across is the book "Unbound; A practical guide to deliverance" by Neal Lozano. It uses 5 "Keys" to walk a person through deliverance. The five keys are 1. Repent, 2. Forgive, 3. Renounce, 4. Command and 5. Blessing. Before going through the 5 Keys of Unbound, it points out that we need to call upon the Holy Spirit and we need to learn to listen to what the Holy Spirit desires to do in our hearts. If we rush into the 5 keys without the Holy Spirit, the 5 keys can become like the keys you have in your junk drawers at home. You know they open something, but you don't know what.

I came across another book that I believe has been instrumental to my healing and deliverance and that is Fr. Michael Gaitley's book "33 Days to Morning Glory." It truly helped me to enter into the truth of who God is and how He loves me. I had based my understanding of God on fallen, sinful and broken people who failed me. When I read Fr. Gaitley's book I felt as if I was meeting God for the first time. The letter that Bl Mother Theresa wrote entitled "I thirst" is a beautiful example of the love of God expressed through Jesus Christ's own thirst on the cross for souls, our soul. **(See Appendix c)**.

In his book Fr. Gaitley shares a method of doing an examination of conscience. This is a way to look at our self-everyday as a means of growing in holiness. What I also noticed is that it seemed to be a lot like Unbound's 5 keys in that it has an element of acknowledging our own sin, asking forgiveness, reconciling ourselves to God, repairing our relationships with others and standing in the love of Christ and Mary to do this.

I would like to show how those that use the examination of conscience taught in the book "33 Days to Morning Glory" could really benefit by incorporating it into the 5 keys taught in the Unbound model of deliverance.

Fr. Michael Gaitley's "B.A.K.E.R. examination of conscience. B is for blessings; A is for Asking, K is for kill, E is for embrace and R is for reconciled. When utilizing the 5 keys of Unbound with BAKER, it becomes even more effective because you can then hear what the Holy

Spirit desire for you to know. Without the Holy Spirit you're just using introspection and "thinking" about your shortcomings or sinful patterns or behaviors. Here is how you begin. Call upon the Holy Spirit. Pray for Him to release the gifts within and through you.

When we invite the Holy Spirit it is a much more gentle way to go into what I like to call the "bad neighborhoods" of our past. There may be many things we need to repent of. Where do we start so we do not get overwhelmed? I heard a Catholic Answers speaker say that our pasts are like bad neighborhoods, you would not want to go in there without some protection or you will get the cr*P beat out of you. So before we go looking at all the places we have failed and come up short or down right sinned, let us first begin by having the Holy Spirit remind us who God is and who we are. So we begin with "B" for blessings.

B=Blessings

We begin by looking at the places in which we have seen the blessings in our lives. We begin with going to the truth and seeing who the Father is and how He has blessed us. This is our "consolations". When our identities have been beaten up through the sinful actions of people who are themselves broken we may be tempted to self-justify because of shame or feelings of unworthiness. We may even misinterpret God's intentions about the circumstances in our lives. We may not believe God desires to share intimate secrets with their hearts and our hearts alone. Whatever the struggles, we must begin with looking to consolations or blessings that we know are true and good as a basis from which to know that all of us are "good" in the eyes of God, faults and all.

A= Ask

Now we call once again upon the Holy Spirit and ask for the Holy Spirit to enlighten our minds as to what God desires for us to know about where there are barriers to Him, or where we are in need of repentance. This is the first Key of the Unbound Model.

KEY 1; Repentance and Faith

When we ask the Holy Spirit He can reveal the root issue instead of the surface things that continue to plague us. For instance, if we have anger issues, raging when things feel out of control or when someone "attacks" our worth, or us we could think our issue is anger. This is how clever the Father of lies is. Anger and rage is a distress symptom of a deeper issue. The Holy Spirit knows the gentlest way to guide you to truth and freedom and He desires to woo His bride gently, He does not desire to kick in your doors or expose you in shame. When we ask Him to lead us to the root, we then can have our hearts moved by His tender Mercy to true repentance.

He can show us that the anger is a reaction to a lie in our heart, an inner vow we have made that locks His healing truth out or perhaps of a judgment we have made about other people or even about God Himself. Anger is a symptom of an idolatry of control. Control is an idol we use to protect ourselves or manage our fears due to powerless wounds or perhaps even fear bonds formed that cause us to believe that God does not save, or He does but will not save us.

When walked through the repentance key, it is so comforting to hear the words of the Prayer team acknowledging and affirming your fear and your deeper desire while at the same time, asking God to forgive you for your judgments, your lack of faith.

"In the name of Jesus Christ, I ask your forgiveness for not believing I could trust you." "Forgive me Jesus for using control as our god instead of coming to you."

This "Asking" is a beautiful way to know what God desires to start with. If we merely think about our shortcomings, our failures and our limitations to love, we will soon despair. When we look at our sin without the Mercy of Jesus Christ and can easily be convinced by the father of lies that we are not forgiven, our sin is too big or perhaps our God will not save us. If we do not ask the Holy Spirit to lead us in this, those that do repent may do it out of shame, fear of judgment or to be "good" rather than to find healing and reconciliation. This will not set the captives free, but causes the lies to dig themselves in deeper. If the root wound is powerlessness and fear, then we find other ways to "control" so as to not open to God. Anger is symptom of an idolatry or false god of control, as a means to self-protect so you see repentance must come from the heart. It is handing the reigns over to Christ, both of them. If we continue to hold onto one of the reigns, we cannot go in the direction God desires to take us in.

KEY 2; Forgiveness

When we ask the Holy Spirit to reveal where we need to forgive we become aware of places we are bound up that we may never have even realized we were not yet set free! He knows all and everything. He knows where pain has caused us to not yet forgiven someone. He knows where we still believe someone does not deserve our forgiveness. He knows where we still desire someone to make atonement for what they did to us. He knows where we are so afraid of dealing with our emotions or anger that we have made unforgiveness and our anger a means to protect our hearts. He sees past false humility to the pride that tries to justify our unforgiveness, He knows where we still do not understand the depths of His ocean of Mercy and He even knows which evil spirits are binding us up of our own free will. The Holy Spirit will gently reveal where we need to forgive, He will lead us there and He will help to set us free.

"In the name of Jesus I forgive my Father for leaving me as a baby and never getting to know me as a daughter. In the name of Jesus I forgive my father for not wanting to be in my life and for not coming to my graduation from high school or college". In the name of Jesus, I forgive my father for not holding my hand, for not holding me in his arms and for not being there to protect me as a child. In the name of Jesus, I forgive my father for not being the father I deserved to have in my life."

Forgiveness is not about giving up your rights, or excusing what someone has done to you. It is about allowing God to work it all out to His better good and glory and relinquishing it's power over you by trusting in the Father. When an intercessor gives you the words, just hearing them said to you out loud is a validation that what was done to you requires forgiveness. When you repeat them, you can feel the healing salve being administered to your heart. It is freeing in that very moment.

K=Kills

What killed or desolated you today? When did your heart drop in your chest from what was done to you or what you had done to someone else? We are not to make major decisions in times of desolation because the father of lies is so good at manipulating our emotions that we are not free to see rightly. When we ask the Holy Spirit to show us the daily desolations, we see where we the wounds of others were at work and it may not have been our cross to carry. We also see the places the enemy is stirring up our emotions to cause us to believe his lies, to make more judgments or vows that separate us from God and in doing so cause us forget that our Father in Heaven knew what He was getting when He made us, we are no surprise to God, yet He so desired us that He willed us into existence despite how He knew we would fail Him. This leads me to the third key.

KEY 3; Renounce

Every day we should be going through B.A.K.E.R. with the 5 Keys of Unbound. When we get to the 3rd key, we need to renounce anything that the Holy Spirit has inspired for us to renounce. Many times we are oppressed by spirts or demons as a means to keep us bound. That is why renouncing lies, vows and even demonic spirits that oppress us is key to deliverance and healing. Fr. Gabriel Amorth, the Vatican's Exorcist writes that diabolical oppressions can be understood by looking to the bible.

'Symptoms vary from a very serious to a mild illness. There is no possession, loss of consciousness, or involuntary action and word. The Bible gives us many examples of oppression; one of them is job, He was not possessed, but he lost his children, his goods, and his health. The bent woman and the deaf and dumb man who were cured by Jesus were not subject to total possession, but there was a demonic presence that caused physical discomfort. Saint Paul was most certainly not possessed by a demon, but he had a demonic oppression that caused an evil affliction: "And to keep me from being too elated by the abundance of revelations, a thorn was given me in the flesh, a messenger of Satan, to harass me" (2 Cor 12:7). There is no doubting the evil origin of the affliction." Fr. Gabriel Amorth
http://www.ignatiusinsight.com/features/framorth_excerpt2_aug04.asp

When we renounce, we break any agreements we have made with the liar and turn our faces back to the Father. We are breaking the ties that bind us. I also believe the renewal of our baptismal vows is a powerful way to renounce the enemy and his lies. It is renouncing Satan, his pomps and works and empty promises.

Many of us have had relationships outside of covenant marriage or have been involved with the occult. There are tarot cards, Ouiji boards, wearing crystals and more. These things must be renounced. Fr. Robert Altier explains Occult Spirits as such;

"These are the things that get in through occult practices. They can be sent or they can be summoned. For instance, if we allow ourselves to be involved in any kind of occult things: playing with a ouija board, going to a palm reader or to a psychic or somebody like that, getting ourselves into any kind of satanic thing. That is how we are going to get these occult spirits. A person can curse you and in doing so a spirit or demon is "sent" to infest you. By infest I mean that it will attempt to harass you with trials, troubles or even manipulate your emotions by sending dark thoughts or feelings to you. The next step would be oppression and this is when it finds a means to attach. Perhaps you agree with lie it presents to you or perhaps you are in mortal sin or maybe you have other habitual venial sins that it can find a toehold from which to attach. Occult spirits are even viler. Because they are occult spirits, they are not very easy to get rid of because they are nasty and tenacious and they fight back, whereas the other ones we can push out. But these are going to cause lots of problems as we try to get rid of them." Fr. Robert Altier Courageous Priest

I want to note that according to Francis McNutt in his book "Deliverance From Evil Spirits" that occult spirits attempt to "block" healing or deliverance ministry sessions. They may manifest as mockery (a person will laugh during a session in inappropriate ways). I mention it as a person may never have dabbled in the occult but when they attempt to receive deliverance they find they are blocked at every turn. This may be the result of an occult spirit that was sent to interfere. There are prayers in this book as well as in Unbound to use to bind up and incapacitate this action of the evil one. Remember what St. Theresa the little flower says about the devil, he is nothing more than a barking dog on a chain. He really is not powerful the only tool he has is fear. Be not afraid and put on your spiritual armor!

For me, renouncing the soul ties also gave me immediate relief. Even the sexual unions we have had outside of marriage can create an unholy tie of our souls to another's. We must renounce these ties, as our souls are to be united with our spouse in Holy Matrimony and no other. Likewise, when we realize that our parents can speak the equivalent of a curse on us when they tell us we are stupid, worthless, selfish and manipulative or by telling us they wish we never born. These are curses because our parents can speak a blessing or curse over us. They have that God given authority over us because they are our parents. In fact, even spouses can speak blessing and curse over one another because they are in covenantal union.

 The book "Unbound" has a step-by-step explanation and guide including the prayers for anyone who desires their own deliverance from the evil ones oppressions in these areas.

Here are some sample prayer for renouncing evil in our lives from Neal Lozano and Neal Anderson to renounce each area of bondage in our mind soul and body. Please buy the book; it will change your life. (Unbound, by Neal Lozano; They Shall Expell Demons, by Neal Anderson. Unbound, by Neal Lozano. Pages 89-90)

Renounce Soul Ties:

If there has been repentance for sexual intimacy outside marriage:

"Father, thank You for forgiving me for the sexual relationship(s) I have confessed and repented. In the name of Jesus, I renounce all sexual and spiritual binding to and I take back the authority I gave to him/her. (or what he/she took from me, if the relationship was not consensual.)"

"In the name of Jesus, I break the power of every spirit behind the soul ties that I have just renounced."

Renounce Every Curse Over Your Life:

"Lord Jesus, I thank You that on the cross You were made a curse, that I might be redeemed from every curse and inherit God's blessing. On that basis, I ask You to release me and set me free to receive the deliverance I need."

"In the name of Jesus Christ, I renounce the curse that _____ spoke over me when (he/she) said _____ ."

"In the name of Jesus Christ, I renounce the curse that I spoke over myself when I said_____ "

"In the name of Jesus Christ, I break the power of the spirit behind each curse that was spoken over me (or that I spoke over myself.)

Thank you, Jesus, for giving me victory over my enemies. I am not afraid. Amen".

"Heavenly Father, there are areas in my life (audibly name the habitual sins such as: unbelief, cold love, fear, pride, un-forgiveness, lust, greed, or any combination of these, as well as the possibility of many others.) that I have not fully surrendered to my Lord, Jesus Christ. Lord, forgive me of compromise. I also ask You for courage to approach the pulling down of strongholds without reluctance or willful deception in my heart. By the power of the Holy Spirit and in the name of Jesus, I bind the satanic influences that are reinforcing compromise and sin within me. I submit myself to the light of the Spirit of Truth to expose the strongholds of sin within me. By the mighty weapons of the Spirit and the Word, I proclaim that each stronghold in my life is coming down! I purpose, by the grace of God, to have only one stronghold within me: the stronghold of the Presence of Christ. I thank You, Lord, for forgiving and cleansing me from all my sins. And by the grace of God, I commit myself to follow through in this area until even the ruins of this stronghold are removed from my mind! Thank You, Father. In Jesus' name. Amen."

4. Authority or Command

"In the name of Jesus Christ, I command every evil spirit and spirits associated to it that I have renounced and every spirit behind the sins I have confessed to leave me right now and go directly to the foot of the cross". "Thank you Jesus for setting me free from the influence of evil spirits. Thank you Father for sending your son to save me." Amen

This is about being set free and Jesus Christ has that authority and power. We, by virtue of our baptism can call upon this power of Jesus Christ and command what we renounce in His name as well as any of the powers and principalities infesting or oppressing us to leave! We need to stand in the authority that we as Christians have been given. Christ said that we would do "all these things and even greater things than this" and He meant it."Truly, truly, I say to you, he who believes in Me, the works that I do, he will do also; and greater works than these he will do; because I go to the Father." John 14:12

Greater works? Yes!!! We will be set free so that we can bring Christ to others so that they too can find healing and freedom!

E=Embrace

When we embrace the love of the Father we embrace the greatness of God's love, the gifts He desires to share with the world through our yes, we embrace the Fathers Blessing. We are called to union and communion with each other but ultimately we have been called to union and communion with God for all eternity in heaven.

5. The Fathers Blessing

Did you know that your name is very important? For all of the years I have traveled and spoke around the country I have noticed that a person's name uniquely reveals how God was revealing himself through their lives as an instrument of His divine will. As I travel I try to tell people (before they told me) what it was that I thought they were doing in ministry based on their name. Not only would I be right but when I was wrong it was not because I was wrong at all but it was because it was on their hearts to do but they had not answered that stirring in their heart. I also noticed that when someone is turned away from God they seem to live the very opposite of their name.

All throughout the bible we are shown that names matter so much that even Paul was renamed to ensure his name matched his calling. Isaac was so named because his mother laughed. All of us have names that were inspired in our parents because of the movements of the Holy Spirit, because our name was written on God's heart before it ever was uttered on our parent's lips. At the moment God names us our name lights up the heavens and flashes like a comet through the stars and throughout the entire universe heralding our goodness as unique and unrepeatable persons with dignity, honor and great worth beyond any price. This is how good precious and good and cherished we are to our Father in Heaven. Many of us have never received words of blessing. I can tell you that if you look to your name, I am sure there is a Father's blessing there for you.

I challenge you to look up your name. If you cannot find the meaning of your name to reveal your call in life then email me because I guarantee I can. What is your confirmation name? I have been told we don't pick our confirmation Saint but that our saint picks us. The Holy Spirit attracts us to that Saint because they will help protect the mission in which we have been chosen to fulfill.

The Fathers blessing is something that all of us should receive and embrace because it heals our wounds; it fills our emptiness and transforms a formless void into something beautiful for God. We have been chosen, we have been called by name.

R=Reconcile

The final examen given by Fr. Gaitley is "reconcile". This is another word for being set free! When our hearts are freed to love we desire to reconcile, to bring healing and freedom to others. When we realize we reacted in a way to self-justify and in doing so hurt someone we love, our first inclination upon healing is to run to them like the prodigal son and say please, please forgive me! I desire to make amends and to restore what was broken between us.

If you have not heard of Unbound I challenge you to discover what has continued to bring me great freedom and healing. If you have not consecrated yourself to Mary I would prayerfully suggest you read my article on why she is the one that helps us to receive our triple portion of the Holy Spirit. If you desire for the Holy Spirit to permeate you, transform you and make you a new creature in Christ, then Mary is the perfect mold from which to pour yourselves into because she formed the body of Christ in her womb.

MY UNDOING

"The pain of purification is called by John of the Cross the "dark night." It is important not to be surprised by the painful moments of our transformation but to know that they're a necessary and blessed part of the whole process." The Fulfillment of All Desire by Dr. Ralph Martin pg 5

I was back in Florida and this time I knew that I was done with my old self. I wanted to be made whole. God's response was to undo me and then put me back together again.

Sometimes it's hard to realize that in order for a house in ruin to be fully restored, it must be torn down so as to begin with a more solid foundation. There is a part of me that feels like this is what Inner Healing has done for me. This form of "therapy" isn't really therapy. It healing. It goes to the foundation and helps to bring about full restoration. I have not been fully restored all at once, but in layers.

"Through many tribulations we must enter the kingdom of God" (Acts 14:22)

I have begun to uncover so many agreements I have made with the "father of lies" and in doing so I had given him and his minions permission to oppress me in so many ways. With inner healing I have been shown that when I am brave enough to trust the builder, my reward will be not just a new and sturdy house but God desires to give me a mansion.

The first thing I had to do was to become vulnerable. That might sound easy when you read the words a crossed the page but for me it was like having the Ren and Stimpy cartoon when they pluck the roots out of the tooth sockets. It was beyond painful.

I felt like someone had stripped me naked in front of a bunch of strangers and I had to stand before them in my nakedness. Then I realized, that I had to go back to the garden and become naked like Adam and Eve were before the fall. If I would be willing to become naked without shame, then I would discover what it truly means to enter into the words "Jesus, I trust in you".

Trust is about being vulnerable. Unless I was willing to be vulnerable, I would never fully enter into trusting God. I thought I trusted God, but I was not relinquishing my control over the direction of my life nor that of my families.

I had come to this retreat to get some healing. I couldn't go home and face all the trials of my life without it! That morning the readings were about "ask and the door will be opened" kind of stuff.

Really? I thought to myself, what a joke. I have been asking for years so where are you? I began to get angry as I listened to scripture saying that God desires to heal us and help us and love us. I guess that means for other people and not for me then. The rage was welling up inside of me. I had to get out of there. The facilitator asked what our reflections were on the readings for the morning. You can bet that I let him have it.

"All the hemorrhaging woman had to do was to touch His garment, what do I have to do?" I screamed.

"Well, the hemorrhaging woman bled for 12 years" said the facilitator.

"Even Lazarus had to wait 3 days before he was raised from the dead" was another response.

"Well, I was sexually abused when I was 3 and I am 41 now so I think I have been waiting long enough" I snapped back.

Their comments, although meant to reassure me, just infuriated me more. For every scripture verse they had to why it was justified that I had not received any relief yet, I had two more as to why God promised

He would show up when He is needed. I left the group and stormed up the stairs to my room. As soon as I got to my room, I let Him have it.

I yelled at God and told Him how upset I was. I went into the bathroom and punched the shower curtain until my knuckles bled (yes, I know it was a temper tantrum).

As I began to lose steam, I yelled out the words; "What do I have to do for you to show up? Lose Control??" That is when I heard the very small words; "yes".

My first thought was; "What? Give up control? Hell No!" What if God doesn't show up? If I am not in control then all hell will break lose (lie)! Is God crazy? It will be a death spiral into chaos (another lie)! Besides, to give up control I would have to be vulnerable. I would have to open myself to the unknown. I can't do that! I am not ready for that! He can't be asking me for that! A better answer would have been, "I cannot do this but you can Jesus, you do this in and through me."

"Vulnerable" is not a word that anyone who has known me would use to describe me. I have prided myself on being self-sufficient. My entire life I have taken care of my family and myself because I felt that no one else could be trusted to do it. The thought of relinquishing control and allowing God to take the reigns terrified me.

As I considered the impending doom that would await me if I even contemplated being vulnerable, I saw an image in my imagination of myself on a horse drawn carriage. I had one rein and God had the other. The carriage was all over the place. I guess letting God have one rein was a great first step but by not giving Him both reigns I was going nowhere fast. I felt the Holy Spirit prompt me to consider giving God both reins, at least for this week so He could show me His plan and that He could be trusted.

Could I do that? Well, I am miserable living the way I am so I have nothing to lose. So I stepped out in fear and consented. I decided anytime I felt Him prompt me, I would submit to being vulnerable. Honestly, I was a little excited to see what this would feel like. I was in a safe place to do this so the circumstances of my experiment seemed worthy of effort.

There is an extraordinary Ted Talk video that a woman at this healing retreat shared with me by Brene Brown entitled "The Power of Vulnerability". It was this video that gave me the courage to embrace vulnerability and then and only then could healing be possible. I should note that she also has a second video that is even better (but needs to be watched after her vulnerability video) entitled "Listening To Shame".

The first morning of my Inner Healing course I would be asked to submit control. I was asked to participate in a living sculpture of the trinity. At one point I was asked to enter into the sculpture. I was asked to rest my head on the "Father's" chest while the " Son" would embrace me from the front and the "Holy Spirit" was supporting and hugging me from behind. It felt awkward and feigned. I began resenting the fact that I had agreed to submit to being vulnerable.

To make matters worse I was sobbing uncontrollably. It felt like everyone watching must surely think I was a basket case and needed psychiatric care (false judgments). I could not express in words what my heart ached with or was crying out so I asked them; "Can I show you what I feel?" The facilitator nodded his head.

I dropped to the floor and lay in a ball in front of the "Father". I held his ankles and laid my face upon his feet. His feet became wet with my tears and wiped them with my hair. The room and the people in it disappeared to me. I remained there sobbing and thought of Mary Magdalene and wished I had expensive perfumed oils to offer. All I could think of was my desire for the Father to love me. I thought to myself, I am not worthy to stand and face you but surely I am worthy to lie at your feet.

There is a great book that describes the scene of Mary Magdalene at Jesus' feet (besides the bible of course) that describes it so very beautifully. It is the book "Love Has a Face" by Michele Perry. In it she describes the scene of Mary Magdalene encountering Jesus as thus:

"She spent her life earning a living by selling false love to any who would buy it. But the Man before her now was different. He looked passed her reputation to her very soul. His eyes had no agenda, no desire to use her. They probed the deepest crevices of her pain but she saw no loathing, no hatred, and no condemnation. How could this be? She saw only compassion and mercy mingled with sadness at what He knew she had suffered. She looked away. She did not know what to do in the face of love that held no guile or hidden motive. Yet her gaze drew back to this Man they called Teacher. Her heart compelled her.

Could it really is true? One more time their gazes locked. She could not look away again even if she tried. How could she return even a drop of the ocean of love in which He washed her that day? It was inappropriate to be sure. It was in the middle of an important dinner for which she had no invitation. And it was not in the proper manner. She could scarcely believe she had just barged right into the middle of the room. It was absolutely undignified yet she was compelled by His love. She washed His feet with her tears and wiped them with her hair. It costs her everything, every shred of dignity and year's wages gone in an instant as she poured out her precious perfume.

Did they know how this amount had been earned? She shuddered at the thought but it was fleeting. The look in His eyes again captured her heart. The room disappeared. The jeering looks and accusations faded as He filled all her vision.

Wasteful. Indignant. Extravagance poured over this Man the only Man who ever showed her the face of love. How could she not pour out her everything on Him? Love outpoured overtook the gathering. The fragrance of intoxicating overpowering adoration that gave all it had and risked all it was filled the room. Inappropriate. Indecent. Scandalous. Wasteful.

But Jesus-what did he do? He accepted it. He defended it. He applauded it. He cherished it. He recorded it for all time." <u>Love has a face</u>, pg 47

I have been praying for receptivity to the Holy Spirit for the past two years. I was now being able to see what vulnerability truly is. It is the predicator to receptivity and this is what I was seeking. Why was I so afraid of vulnerability? Why did I see vulnerability as weakness? After all God had brought me through so much healing. Why was I still resisting Him? It was then that I got the answer. I saw a picture in my mind of me at 3 years of age being molested by the babysitter.

This is when the biggest lie of them all was undone. I had made the agreement that vulnerability means losing your rights and being unprotected. You cannot get more vulnerable than being three years old, naked and being sexually assaulted in a strange place. Even if I could have gotten away where would I have gone? I was alone and had no idea how to get home. This was vulnerability to me. I had decided at three years old that being vulnerable meant being violated, assaulted and victimized. I thought the only person that could be trusted to protect me was myself because others cannot be counted upon. It was this lie that I had decided to believe that set me up to be a woman that could not be vulnerable. I had misunderstood what being vulnerable means. I had thought to be a vulnerable woman would mean I had to become a woman that was weak and that was something I was hardwired against. God had put strength in my heart and the liar had led me to believe being vulnerable meant I had to give that up and become weak.

Mary Magdalene was not weak she was brave. She was brave enough to believe that Christ would accept her and her offering. She marched a crossed that floor and she opened herself in a very vulnerable way. She was not assaulted there nor did she become violated. In fact, it was her lifestyle that violated her and stripped her of her dignity. Here, in her willingness to expose herself she was having her dignity restored. That's when it hit me. If I was willing to become naked in the same way then could I be healed too?

Was I resisting being vulnerability because I was still consumed by shame? What is shame? What does it mean to say that Adam and Eve were naked without shame? Could it be that I must be willing to become naked in front of God so that in that voluntary vulnerability I could finally experience healing?

The answer was yes. Yes I needed to relinquish control so that I could let God lead me. If I could do that, it would be the beginning of learning to trust Him.

Control has been my lover for the last 41 years. It has made me feel strong, competent and has soothed my anxieties like drugs for a junkie. If I could not deal with something happening in my life, I would take control. If you want to know how that worked out for me, lets just say I have burned a lot of bridges in my life using control as a coping mechanism. Being vulnerable meant I would have to give up control and learn to trust God with my life. This was going to be harder than I thought but God did not abandon me.

One of the nights I was at the Healing retreat I had a dream about what this control was doing in my marriage. In the dream I was about to be attacked by a large deformed dog. It was about to crush my skull in it's oversized jaws. My husband was standing in front of me, raising his fist to strike the dog beast down. I watched, as he seemed to be slowly puffed up with air. He was getting larger and larger the way a balloon is inflated with helium but he did not release his raised fist to strike the dog. Fear began to well up inside of me as considered he may be too late and I doubted his ability to save me. I had to take over. I began to scream at him.

"What are you doing? I screamed at him as loud as could. "Hit the dog!!! He is going to kill me! Shawn! What's wrong with you? Hit the dog!" I screamed over and over.

As I continued to yell at him, I watched as the air began to go out of him and he grew smaller and smaller with every one of my screams. The next thing I knew I was no longer being threated but my 8-year-old daughter had taken my place. Her tiny, petite body, the little flibbertigibbet of a girl that she is coward as the dog loomed over her ready to consume her within it's powerful jaws. I looked at Shawn; surely he would rise to the occasion for his daughter? I sat powerless to help her and watched, as my husband once again grew larger and larger as if filling with air. He grew larger and larger and I watched as his fist rose up higher and larger. My fear that the dog would strike before Shawn would act burst out of me again. I began to yell and holler at him to hit the dog. The louder I yelled, the smaller my husband became. Then I woke up.

The next morning I thought about the dream. I asked the Holy Spirit what my dream meant. Then I understood. I understood that my desire to control as well as my refusal to be vulnerable was emasculating my husband. I had stripped him of feeling adequate, worthy or even capable of doing, well...anything much less be a protector to the family.

Could it be that my controlling the family and making all of the decision was stealing his joy, his purpose, and his worthiness? If he were in that role, would he in fact become a more beautiful husband and father? I then thought about how the man is the "head" and the woman is the "heart". I honestly believe that for a woman to operate in the head, she must make her heart covered in stone. A woman is made to flow from the heart. Even scientists and psychiatrists will tell you that a man has the ability to think through stressful situations and assess them cognitively without being drawn into the affect. He can then compartmentalize them and rank them in according to purpose and then deal with the decisions that flow from it.

Women usually think on things simultaneously. For me to put myself into the very stressful role of dealing with all of the difficult decisions (that come from the head) I had to shut off my heart or else I would have internally combusted. I had made my heart into stone. No wonder I had a hard time hugging and kissing my children! I had to turn off the affect so I could get things done! I had a house to run and finances to sort out and decisions to make and stress to deal with! I had no time for snuggling and comfort children.

It' somewhat ironic that I went to Florida to find out why I have a hard time showing affection and ended up dealing with the very thing that was the root or cause. I thought about how arguing with the HVAC guy or electrical guy or the bank guy etc., was making me into a hardened woman not a vulnerable one. I could not be both. I was not made for being a manipulative woman that always found a way to get what she wanted or needed. I was made to love and be loved.

I now had to ask myself the question is there a spiritual aspect of this issue of mine that must be addressed? "Have I come into agreement with a spirit of control?" I looked deeply within me and prayed to the Holy Spirit for wisdom. I had barely begun to ask the question when a resounding YES rang out within me. Its name is The Jezebel Spirit.

The next day I spent some time with the Intercessory Prayer team and we renounced lies, unbound agreements and cut the connections that the Jezebel Spirit had made to me. I realized right away that I had come into agreement with the clever lies it had proposed to me. It is in making an agreement that I had given it power in my life. I can honestly say I experienced a tremendous shift in my thinking and freedom from something very powerful. That week was another week in the journey to becoming the woman I have always been meant to be. If I want my husband to succeed in being father, husband and man of God that he has been called to be, then I must give him the opportunity to lead our family. It is this very thing that will fulfill him and his masculinity.

So where am I now? Well, now I am dealing with trust and overcoming the fear that wells up inside of me when I am not the one making the decisions at home or orchestrating how the days, weeks and months play out (not easy at all but I can do all things through Christ Who Strengthens me! Phil 4:13). The evil one knows my weak areas so now I must be alert for his attempts to poke me there with his pitchfork. Remember, we can be healed in an area but we must work at acquiring the maturity.

Everyday it hurts. Everyday I am challenged to be vulnerable but the first step came in understanding that Jesus would never define being vulnerable as opening myself to be violated.

Being vulnerable now means that I am willing to be imperfect. I know that I am not bad, in fact, I am the opposite, and I am very, very good. I may make mistakes and do things that are bad, but I am not bad. I will continue to struggle against the difficulties of life but now I realize that when I am vulnerable, I open up the door for God to come in and take care of me.

I have now entered into a trusting relationship with God in a very different way. I try to pay attention to when I use the words "should" and "need" and "but" because they show me when I am trying to control people or things or when I am not allowing God the freedom to move in my life or the lives of others. It important to identify what triggers you. This will help you in the battle.

I am glad I had the courage to be vulnerable because if I hadn't I would have missed a week of intense inner healing of the deep wounds I have carried from my childhood. I am not all better yet, but I am on the road to healing. He knocked on the door and I opened it. I now allow Him to lead as the Good Shepard and I am continually reminding myself not to take the place of the butcher (the guy who drives the sheep). When He leads (and I am not driving things from behind) then I can trust that He will take care of me and I can be vulnerable. His way, affords protection, green pastures, quiet waters, it refreshes my soul and I am protected from evil. That sounds a whole lot better than what I have been giving myself the past 40+ years.

God reminded me that when someone has identity wounds and shame they are cut off from God and feel unworthy of love. He reminded me that we wound in the way we wounded. All of a sudden I realized that my husband felt rejected by me all of the time because he had rejection wounds. The real maturity came when I understood that we are called to be Christ to one another.

For so long would get angry and yell to my husband that I cannot be God to him when in fact that is exactly what we are called to do. I have been so blessed to have a husband so utterly in love with me. He has always been so trusting of my "goodness." This is another gift to me.

A wife can sanctify her husband and a husband can sanctify his wife. I desire to be brave enough to find continued healing so that I may become a tabernacle, a monstrance from which to radiate the love of Christ to others, especially my husband who has his own wounds. It was with this desire that I realized I was gaining the maturity in my new found freedom. I no longer saw something being expected or taken from me, I saw that I was a gift to be given to an other and out of my deep and sincere love for him I desired to be gift to him and to inspire the feelings of worthiness in him to do the same.

What an amazing privilege to have a husband that would allow me to reveal the love of Christ to him. If I could look upon him in love, affirm his identity and show him love just for his own sake then I could help bring healing to his wounds and one day he may feel worthy enough to look up to the father himself. I had others help me to feel worthy; perhaps I can do the same for him.

What happened next continues to astound me. His whole countenance changed. He went from looking pained and like he would drown without me to looking at me in the same loving and affirming way I was making an effort to show him. Then I found myself looking at him in this way of just "beholding." It came from so deep inside of me that I just looked at him like this without trying. What happened next was unexpected. He began to behold me in the same way. After 20 years of marriage I have entered into an intimacy with him that I have never known and I have been utterly undone.

FREEDOM AND MATURITY

> *"God wants you to be free. He wants to heal you—spirit, soul and body. However, we can never be completely free and healed until we forgive. Forgiveness is the foundation for all healing. ... Many times forgiveness is also accompanied by hate, resentment, revenge, anger and bitterness. If we allow these negative emotions to remain in our spirits, we perhaps will end up with a physical problem such as arthritis, high blood pressure, stomach problems, colitis or heart problems."*
> Betty Tapscott and Fr. Robert De Grandis, Forgiveness and Inner Healing, page 1

I remember reading a book on training kids to behave and it said that because kids process information differently than we do. They visualize a lot of what we say. If a child is running and you want them to stop say, "Walk" instead of "stop running". If you say, "stop running" it takes their brains longer to process the command. They must first associate that you said running and they are running. Then they must realize you want them not to be running. However, if you say, "walk" they will sometimes begin walking while they are still processing the command as their brains are already understanding it.

There are two points I want to make with this. First of all it is that the way in which wounded people see and hear the world is much different than a person who was given a healthy and affirming childhood. Secondly it is that we must walk before we run.

The childhood song of "Sticks and stones will break my bones but words will never hurt me" is just not true. In fact, because I am body and soul, words will have its effects in and with my body just like throwing stones at me will hurt my dignity.

Our words are just as powerful as stones and it is essential that we govern them. What we says matters and we can bless or curse one another with our words. When we use words to curse our own children it has devastating and sometimes long lasting consequences.

I have had to listen differently than before to make sure that what people are saying is not different than what I heard.

When we have identity wounds we can take offense at something not intended to offend us. It is not that we need to develop a thicker skin, this would in fact be a hardening of our hearts and is the worst thing we could do to! We must be vigilant against the hardening of our hearts.

Most people who have hardened hearts have underneath it the most fragile of identities. I was like a porcupine. If I felt threatened, my quills came out. Underneath it all I am the most soft and easygoing person that is easily moved to compassion and tears.

To elaborate on the second point, being healed does not always mean being cured. In fact, because we live in a fallen world with fallen people with fallen natures the likelihood that we will continue to hurt others and be hurt is probably great but the difference is that when we find healing we find freedom. We find freedom to love and be loved. We find freedom to live our lives and we find truth for the first time ever. Imagine our wounds were like a broken leg, when we find healing we can walk again but that does not mean we are ready to run a marathon.

When we begin to heal and find freedom the temptation can be to think we can run. When we fall in an area we thought was healed the temptation can be to think we were never healed in the first place and fear that all the work we have done in our lives will be undone and our peace will disappear. This is not true. Just because we cannot run does not mean our healing was not genuine. When I returned home from Florida I forgot that I should not run but that I should walk. I also had a tremendous introduction to the Heart of the Father and His love and concern for me.

Some of the first tastes of freedom came when I began addressing father wounds created by my stepfather.

One of the obstacles I faced in being able to go to God the Father for my identity was my own father wounds. Have you ever heard the saying "You can't give what you don't have?" It makes sense doesn't it? I can't give you a dollar if I don't have a dollar. But in terms of affection, love and relationships it makes even more sense. I could not find the restoration and forgiveness from God the Father until I forgave those that "trespassed against me".

> *Wounds from early childhood are often the deepest roots that need healing "We have made frequent reference to the healing of father memories. This is because the scars of an unloving father relationship are so much at the root of other problems. Normally children are introduced to God as Father. If 'Father' means judgment, punishment, distance and abandonment, then the child accepts God as such. Therefore a lifetime of spiritual activity can be built on a sick foundation. ... The person accepts neither that God loves him nor that intimacy and union with God are possible."* Francis MacNutt, Healing, page 147

I am in no way excusing the abusers in my life, but unless I was willing to forgive them I would never truly be freed from the wounds they caused in me and would most probably continue to engage in attempts to numb my own pain. I would also need to discover God the Father's love for me. I was tired of this cycle in which I was constantly a victim and I wanted a change.

Although someone else's sin caused my abuse it was my decision to sin as a response to it and until I acknowledged those areas of my life I was in need of forgiveness I could not find the courage or strength to forgive others.

I knew it was a very dangerous thing to look at my sins without first having a relationship with Jesus Christ. Without Christ's mercy I would only see shame, judgment and condemnation for how I chose to run away from my pain. I had used many false idols to resist being vulnerable and trusting in Him. I tried to do it myself which ultimately led me into darker sin which hardened my heart to those in my life, even my own children who needed me the most.

With the help of a merciful and loving Christ I had the courage to press into the wounds and ask for forgiveness. It was then that He led me to the Heart of the Father and it was there my identity began to heal my whole "person".

The gift of forgiveness is freedom. It sounds so understated and to see the sentence on the page I cannot help but feel I am not giving it due credit. Freedom is everything. When we are bound up by sin we are unable to love or be loved. We are unable to see truth or be truthful. We are unable to live a life in freedom we are dying a slow death of bondage to our sin.

Forgiveness is so powerful that when we accept it for ourselves it is as if the Holy Spirit, the healer and great physician begins to suck the venom and poison out of our lives. Its effect is real and immediate and the taste of freedom gives you the strength and courage to press on.

My only desire is for my continued healing and for my family to find healing as well. I want them to find the freedom and joy and happiness in life that God desires for them. I know from experience that freedom only comes when we are willing to face the truth and feel the weight of the cross that all of us must carry. We cannot do it without a relationship with Jesus Christ, to do so would incapacitate someone, it would destroy him or her.

My first prayer for those who do not know Jesus Christ is that you ask for Him to come into your heart and show himself to you. God's goodness is not limited by our comprehension of Him and often times we have been let down by so many people in our lives we can believe or feel like God will also let us down. Dig down deep inside of the place that wants healing and beg God the Father to help you step out in trust of Him. He will not abandon you!

Let my witness prove that He exists and that you too are worthy. If this too is hard for you to begin with then pray that Jesus Christ bring you a grace of feeling worthy. All it takes is a mustard seed of desire and that is the spark of receptivity He needs to set your heart on fire for him and his desire is that you were already set ablaze.

If your father was not affectionate, you may have trouble showing affection to your own children. If your father never played ball with you, you probably did not know how to play ball very well. If your father did not have the resources to draw upon to be the father you deserved, then it may be true that you also have limited resources. This is true for our parents and for us as well.

So many of us have wounds even those of us who were not sexually abused. There are so many places our own parents that could have been wounded and this forms the person they became. Is it no wonder then that some parents could not give us what we deserved because having never received it themselves, they have no idea how to give it to anyone else?

Thanks to my growing awareness of this fact as well as my continued understanding of what Divine Mercy is, I have realized that my parents did not give me the childhood I deserved because they also did not get it.

This is becomes glaringly apparent when I contemplate my stepfather's childhood. From the stories I have heard growing up he was raised by a mother who not only abandoned him, but also a mother who subjected him to things I will not mention here but will say they may have been worse than anything I had to endure. My mother, thou imperfectly, did love me and tried to give me the best and do the best for me. This poor little boy, was given nothing to teach him about his value, his worth being made in the image and likeness of God. He never heard how his gifts and talents could change the world. He was never loved for just being himself. Instead, he grew up devoid of affection and the affection he did witness before she finally abandoned him all together was pornographic.

So you see, the anger, hurt and hate have begun to melt away. As a mother of 3 boys, I have become acutely aware of how boys not only adore their mothers but they often times say they want to marry their mothers. My stepfather was stripped from the love his little boy heart needed as nourishment and instead his soul was starved. Thinking about him as a little boy really created a startling realization in my heart. This man was a baby once, he was a toddler and he was a little boy who needed love and affection but instead he was abused and abandoned. It makes it easier to contemplate forgiveness when we can separate out the sin from the person God created. God does not create monsters. The enemy, through sin does that.

Until the wound is addressed, it will continue to fester and poison and ultimately lead to spiritual death. I had wanted to write him a letter for years. In fact over the years I have written many letters but only recently did I have the courage to mail one. Writing the letter was great therapy as well but at some point if we really want to be released from the bondage the abuse creates in us we must forgive.

The day finally came. I wrote a letter to my stepfather. I told him all these things and my mother heart shared how he had deserved to be loved and cherished by his mother. I apologized, yes, apologized for the women in his life who had hurt him and had failed to tell him that he was made in the image and likeness of God and that he did nothing to deserve this God given dignity, but that it was a gift from God who loved him beyond measure. I then forgave him for all the wrongs that he had done, telling him that I understood how you couldn't give what you do not receive.

I then told him that my motivation in doing this was his salvation. I told him that I did not want him to go through life thinking that someone like him did not deserve to be loved by God. I knew if the devil could convince him of this then his soul would be at stake.

Let me very clear about something. It took me almost 30 years to get to this place. It was a process. I am not telling anyone that they should do this but rather I am sharing my own experience of how I was able to come to place in which I honestly desired to forgive my abuser. The book "Left To Tell" by Imaculee Illibigeza was a huge catalyst in being able to even contemplate true forgiveness.

She is the woman who survived the slaughter of millions of Rwanda citizens during the genocide by hiding for several months with several other women in a small bathroom. She hid there while listening to the screams of her family and friends as they were run down and slaughtered with machetes. Her story opened my eyes to just how and how powerful and healing forgiveness can be and how poisonous it can be to our soul when we do not forgive.

The devil is clever. He can keep someone from going to church and asking forgiveness by convincing us that God is too good and does not "like" sinners as bad as us. I did not want this to be the lie my step-father would believe and knew the only *person* he could receive or believe this from, to prove to him he could be worthy of God's forgiveness would be the child he abused. That person was I.

I then told this man, who was my step-father from age 4 to 14, that he must believe that God loves him and desires union and communion with him because I would be the one person who had every right to suggest otherwise. If I was saying it, I told him, then he must consider the fact that it is true.

I did not want the enemy using me as a reason to keep this man's soul from God. As far as I was concerned, I was going to allow God to use my mercy as a conduit of grace.

A few weeks later I was at my brother's house. His father (my step-father) stopped by to talk to him. When he was at the door, he saw me inside and asked if he could speak to me outside.

His voice was all humility and gentleness. I had not talked with my stepfather for over 25 years. I was scared, but I went out to speak to him. He thanked me for the letter and for the first time in over two decades, I was given an apology for what he had done. He was so thankful, so grateful that when he walked away, he looked taller somehow.

I can only imagine the feelings of betrayal someone might have that was abused by their own father or even a priest. I will not suggest that I am either superior or better than another for offering forgiveness to my abuser.

However, I would gently urge anyone reading this who has suffered the pain and anguish of abuse to consider what forgiveness will offer them. It will bring you freedom. It brings freedom in ways I could not explain because it must be experienced.

The way to begin is simple. Just by asking God to plant a mustard seed of desire "to want to forgive" is the best way to start. It is a beautiful prayer. "Jesus, give me the desire to want to forgive".

Not all are ready to do what I did, in fact the only thing I am sure of is that this was something I was called to do and by no means is it a template for others. That is between God and yourself. For me, realizing how many times I have failed my own kids has helped to become compassionate towards those who failed me. We cannot prevent hurting our own children but we can work on cleaning our own hearts our so that we can love better and more rightly.

We are all going to fall short of the Glory of God. We will all fall short in being the perfect parent, the difference will be that we have our eyes open and desire to heal and change our hearts so that in healing our wounds we trust God more and we pass less woundedness to our children and more of His love.

SETTING BOUNDARIES

Some of you might desire to forgive and even let your abuser know. It is important that you pray about this carefully before acting upon it or to even seek spiritual counseling.

There are some abusers who no matter how much you try to love them will only use that opportunity to inflict more pain on you because of their great woundedness.

There are some mothers or fathers that no matter how many times you try to have a relationship with them, they will continue to reject you.

How are we to respond? The answer is in the gospel of St. Luke " Love your enemies," he referred right afterwards to actions; "Do good to those who hate you". (Lk. 6:27)

Whatever your circumstance is, just invite God in and pray about what if anything you are being called to do before acting or you may be in for more pain. There is such thing as healthy boundaries. Someone reminded me recently that there is a difference between forgiveness and reconciling. I have forgiven my parents for where they have failed me but we have yet to reconcile our relationship.

Write a letter or maybe write several letters. Take it before the lord and ask Him to heal those places in your heart that he stirs up and draws your attention to, as he often will reveal more layers that he desires to heal within your heart. Whatever the journey, forgiveness is another beautiful way to bring deeper healing within you and with God.

> *"Genuine Forgiveness usually comes only after we grieve the loss, express our anger, and are freed from the damaging message of the wrong done to us. Only when we gain a restored sense of self can we forgive in a real and healthy way. Only then, can we truly let go of the message of a memory that damaged us, which is what forgiveness is all about."*
> -Greg Boyd, Seeing is believes, page 123

EMBRACING GREATNESS: The New Evangelization

"Go into all the world and preach the gospel to the whole creation. He who believes and is baptized will be saved; but he who does not believe will be condemned. And these signs will accompany those who believe: in my name they will cast out demons; they will speak in new tongues; . . . . . they will lay their hands on the sick, and they will recover." Mark 16:15-18

So what do we do next once we find healing and are made whole? We are to become like stars. As a young child I was always attracted to stars. I even thought that deep down inside of me I heard a still soft voice that I was going to become a star. I do not mean I thought I would be an actress; in fact I am not sure I knew what it meant. What I understood was that there was something about stars that I felt connected to. During my rebellious period in college I even got a tattoo of a star.

What I now understand is that we are all to become like stars. We are to become like the star of Bethlehem. The Star of Bethlehem was a light in the darkness that guided men to God. We too are to become like this star. We are to shine like a light in the darkness and lead humanity to God. It is not good to receive for just us. We are made for relationship. We are made for union and communion. We must share what we have been given with others. St. Ignatius said something like, we are to be filled not for our own sake but so that when we are filled we may overflow and splash onto those around us. I like the analogy I have used before which is the image of us being a chalice and that when we are healed, the grace that pours into us is retained and we can bring a drink of it to others that thirst.

I have heard some people say the worse way to die is to die of thirst. I imagine the same is true of spiritual thirst. When we embrace our greatness it is because we are embracing our true identities. Our great dignity comes from God and when we embrace it we are embracing Him. We then become like a tabernacles, carrying within us the light of Christ. We are to bring Christ to others through our hands and our feet. We are to radiate something so magnificent that they cannot help but to I have heard some people say the worse way to die is to die of thirst. I imagine the same is true of spiritual thirst. See His Truth, His Life and His love.

It is this greatness that has enabled me to write this book and to speak all over the globe on issues that I used to feel I had to hide from the world. It is in embracing our greatness as sons and daughters of God that we become transformed and made whole. When we are free to love and be loved by God the Father then we are able to become like Christ to others. It reflects from our faces as if those who encounter us are experiencing the living God in our own presence. It is in this encounter that they begin to long for Him.

It is not because of anything we do or say, but rather it is that they see what happens when people open themselves to God. They see that in opening ourselves to receive Him deep within our hearts He conceives divine life within us. They are able to encounter Him because we make visible the invisible truth that God makes all things new.

The star of Bethlehem guided those seeking for truth to the one true God. We live in a world where everyday there are people seeking to be filled and the only thing that can make them whole is God. In fact, that desires, that ache, that hunger, was infused into them at the moment of their conception so that they would always reach outside of themself to be completed by the one and only thing that will satisfy. That "thing" is not a thing it is God and He reveals that He is, in and through the mystery of the trinity, Father, Son and Holy Spirit.

How do we become a star of Bethlehem? We first have to receive Him ourselves. We must first desire to be made whole and know, love and serve Him so that we can be in union and communion with him in this world and in the next.

God knows all the places we have failed him and will fail him and yet he created us anyways. Out of all of the potential people God could've created we were chosen to be created and to come into the world to exist in fact of this very particular time in history.

But it gets better than this! God is calling all of us to enter into the redemption of the world! God could have chose to redeem the world anyway he liked. What he decided was that he wanted all of us to enter into this great work with him.

He does this by transforming our wounds much like his own were from the power of the cross. His "cracks" were in fact the greatest gift given to the entire world. Our wounds, our cracks, our inadequacies become the very place, once transformed like a firing kiln to a clay pot, becomes the very form from which God can best shine through, pour out of and be given to others. He is magnified by our smallness and our weakness.

God is calling you and is issuing a marriage proposal in which He desires to transform you and touch the lives of those around you through your fiat.

A treasure in earthen vessels is about our unique and unrepeatable personhood, it is about our immortal soul chosen by God to be called into existence. The earthen vessel reveals that the person we are is feminine or masculine and also is a sign that we are called to love like the trinity.

We are to bring Christ to the world with our own hands and feet, with our own stories. Each of our stories is as unique as our fingertips, as unique as our personhood. We are the vessel and form helps us to tell the story of who Christ is and who we are in Christ. We should never underestimate the power of conversion to work through even the most broken of vessels.

Lazarus is an example of just such a vessel. He was dead. A rotting corpse and according to chief mourners "stinking" and yet when Christ shone through Lazarus, an entire city and now every generation to come, was converted through his story and through his form. For me, my form is the reed. I have been hallowed out, whittled and cut into. The story I have to tell is of being transformed through my children and my husband and most certainly through the healing power of Jesus Christ. This is the piper's breath that blows through the reed turning a mere reed into a beautiful musical instrument. I've been able to identify specific attributes or virtues that God has helped to develop in me for each one of my children.

For Maegan it was my first taste of vulnerability and being selfless. For Sarah it was receiving the selfless love of my husband. For Elisha it was an invitation to see how important it is to be affirmed and to affirm others especially with physical affection. For Gabriel it was submission, to submit to something that God asked of me even when it was hard. For AnnaMarie it was learning to love when it is difficult to love and when life is hard. For Mercedes it was learning about trusting in His Mercy. For Christopher it was seeing how radiating joy transforms hearts. For Jonah it was persevering despite difficulties and hardships because the reward is sweet.

For each child I have received a healing of a major wound, crack, or notch that was cut into me by sin. God transformed it and the grace He has given to me in each of these areas has brought me freedom to love more rightly and the results is what all of us are called to be, an icon of love.

Each time I was cracked, wounded or cut into because of my sin or the sin of others, the enemy proposed a lie so to enter into my heart and bring me to a place of shame and keep me locked up there with my pain being the jailor and my fear the jail cell.

God the Father loves you so much that there is no battle he will not fight to come and find you no matter how high the tower you may be locked up in. Christ is like Mel Gibson in Braveheart and there is no enemy he will not fight to free you. The Holy Spirit wants to expose the lies and bring healing to your wounded hearts and when you become vulnerable and allow Him in to truly see you, Christ will transforms your wounds into stained glass windows illuminating and radiating God's beauty, God's light, God's truth to the world in and through your story. If you're scared but want this freedom then begin simply with the words "Jesus, I trust in you". The words taught by Jesus to St. Faustina in the message of Divine Mercy. These 5 words are a powerful prayer and will no go unanswered if you pray them everyday.

"I can do all things through Christ who strengthens me" Philippians 4:13

Nothing is impossible with God and you can do all things through Christ. If you still are not sure then try the words "Jesus, I can not do this but you can, Jesus be my strength" or even the words "Come Holy Spirit, Come". No elaborate prayers are necessary to begin. God knew what he was getting when he made you.

You are no surprise to God and yet in brining you in the world you can be sure that you are most certainly wanted and most certainly good enough to come as you are. He does not need you to be holy before approaching him. Would you deny your child because they are covered chocolate mess from eating all of the cookies despite being told no? No, instead, it is in their willingness to come, as they are that we delight in them all the more. Be not afraid and come as you are.

*"You have been made for greatness.."*St. John Paul II

They will know us by our joy they will know us by our love. We are called to transformation. The new evangelization is about allowing Christ to permeate us. We embrace our greatness when we dare to take what we know in our heads and connect it to our hearts. When we move from knowing God, to being in an intimate relationship with Him.

When we allow ourselves to truly be seen and to really see the person God puts in front of us everyday is when we enter into one another's story of redemption. God works through cracked pots, because His greatness is magnified in our weakness. The truth is that the enemy puts salt in our wounds because he is terrified that if we actually go into the wounds and bring Christ there with us, we would discover that when Christ redeems them, they become like jewels in the Crown of the creator.

I am a person who was sexually abused. I decided to write a book about healing from sexual abuse because I know the ache. I know the pain. Christ can shine from this broken place in me and now my brokenness is made beautiful.

Put your fingers into my wounds and see the glory of Jesus Christ and allow Him to resurrect you! Come from the tomb that you are waiting in, more dead than alive and see the Glory of God. You have been created for a reason and God desires for you to enter into the redemption of the world with Him. He wants you to bring your emptiness to Him so that He can fill it and pour Himself out to others. Will you say yes?

With your Yes, he will begin a might work in and through you. When we receive Him, He begins to conceive within us a transformation of love. We then are to ask the Holy Spirit to release the operational gifts of the Holy Spirit given to us at baptism and confirmation. These are what will make the person in front of us KNOW that God is real and seeking them out PERSONALLY.

When we speaks prophetic words, or words of knowledge, exhortation, wisdom, tongues or their interpretation we emanate like a light, we radiate Him and that is what will draw humanity to Him. Like St. John in his mother's womb, deep within their own hearts there will be a leaping for joy as well as a reverent bow within them as they realize they have encountered the power of the living God. Begin simply; just say yes to greatest marriage proposal you will ever get.

"Lord, I am not worthy that you should enter under my roof, but only say the word and my soul shall be healed."

The New Evangelization begins within each one of us. It is about being transformed. "People are not interested in hearing about Jesus, they want to see Jesus." Bl Pope John Paul II

I am a new creation in Christ. I still find myself amazed at the transformation. People who have not seen me for years tell me that I am like a different person.

I tell them that if grace perfects our natures, then I am not a different person, rather I am more capable of revealing the person God has made me to be.

I am a treasure in an earthly vessel and my life has created the form best able to reveal a call to love and to be loved from the bridegroom to His bride. All it took was for me to give my "fiat" which has become the greatest "I DO" I have ever uttered.

Appendix A

Pictures of Me

Top Left: Me at age 3, the year I was first sexually abused.

Top Middle: Age 10, The year my step-Father began to abuse me

Top Right: Age 11, Just before my first communion I finally told and experienced an amazing "God Moment" from which I believed there is a God and He wanted to help .

Middle Left: The year I was put into foster Care

Middle Middle: My freshmen year in High-School living my life as an object for use.

Middle Right: The year my husband and I married.

Bottom Left: Charlie and Susan at The Theology of The Body Institute

Bottom Middle: Christopher West and I at the Theology of The Body Institute

Bottom Right: Me Before abuse and Me this year on my 43rd birthday.

Appendix B

Healing Resources

Heart of the Father Ministries
www.HeartOfTheFather.com

Heart of the Father is a deliverance ministry based in Ardmore, PA, led by Neal and Janet Lozano.

The ministry focus is empowering people to reclaim their true identity in Christ as sons and daughters of the Father through Unbound Ministry. We are dedicated to equipping people throughout the world to take hold of the freedom that they have been given in Jesus Christ, and to help others do the same. **Books: "Unbound" and "Resisting The Devil"**

"The Healing Of Families"
www.HealingOfFamilies.com
by Fr. Yozefu-B. Ssemakula

Fr. Ssemakula presents a simple, effective, and powerful prayer method for freeing you and your family from problems you have prayed about for a long time without results, including health issues. Through Father's inspired book and seminar you will learn to distinguish between the true Cross of Christ that we have to carry for our salvation, Mt 16:24 (necessary suffering), and the false Cross, which is a simple captivity and oppression of God's children, LK 4:18 (unnecessary suffering). God never wills evil and pain for us at any point in our lives. Evil and pain are interruptions of God's plan for our lives Jer 29:11, even if good can be extracted from them. 1 John 4:8 tells us: "God is love." John 10:10 states: "I came that they might have life and have in abundantly." God's will is always good. When things turn out bad for us, it can never be the will of God.
www.HealingOfFamilies.com

John Paul II Healing Center www.JPIIHealingCenter.org

Inspired by the life and teaching of Blessed John Paul II, we are dedicated to healing broken hearts and restoring the image of God in the human person, as represented most fully by the hearts of Jesus and Mary.

Book: "Be Healed" by Dr. Bob Schuchts (Ave Maria Press)

Theology of The Body Institute
www.TobInstitute.org

Theology of the Body Institute envisions a world filled with men and women who freely embrace God's glorious plan for their sexuality. Only from this foundation can an authentic culture of life and love take root and flourish. We aim to ensure that the teachings of John Paul II are promoted faithfully and effectively. Through our first rate education and unique outreach programs, the TOB Institute will be a premiere resource for education and formation in Theology of the Body.

Dr. Conrad Baars www.ConradBaars.com

Born Only Once

Feeling and Healing Your Emotions

Healing The Unaffirmed

33 Days To Morning Glory www.AllHeartsAFire.org

This book and workbook will help you to set your hearts on fire with love of God and neighbor and to inspire us to works of mercy in our families, parishes, and communities.

Appendix C

Wounds Chart: I created this chart by using concepts taught at the Course "Sexual Healing and Redemption: Restoring The Glory by Dr. Bob Schuchts to make it easier to identify the core wounds. My Wounds:

SIN	IDOL/ WORSHIP OF	ROOT WOUND	INNER VOWS &	IDENTITY LIE	DISTRESS SYMPTOMS
PRIDE	SELF	SHAME: Identity Wound (Neglect, trauma Abuse)	"I must prove my worth" I will use vanity or intelli or success to show people I am valuable	"I am Unworthy" "I am stupid or ugly" "I am bad or dirty" I have not value	Self-Justification, Self-Pity, Self-criticism, selfish, conceited, vain, lying, exageration, blame others, name dropper, work-aholic, rebellious, disobedient, neurotic, self-obsessed.
ENVY	STATUS	Affirmation-deprivation (neglect)	I must bring others down so that I can feel good about myself I will use people	People are fake I never get what I deserve	Jealousy, gossip, slander, bitterness, victim
GREED	POSESSIONS	FEAR BONDS MISTRUST MOTHER-WOUNDS	I must hoard my money, possesions, etc I wont rely on anyone or anything	"I canot trust People," I cannot trust God "If I trust, I will hurt."	hoarding, lack of emotional connection dissassociative issues, passive aggressive unassertive, difficulty w/intimacy or giving or showing attention or saying thank you
GLUTTONY	SUBSTANCE FOR PLEASURE	HOPELESSNESS LACK OF AFFECTION OR AFFIRMATION	I will numb myself when I get overwhelm I will turn to pleasure when I'm hurting insid	I cant change Nothing I do matters "the addiction will numb my pain"	(Gluttony and Sloth often Connected) excessive fatigue, lack of discipline, easily overwhelmed
SLOTH	BODILY COMFORT to avoid suffering	POWERLESS AND OR CONFUSION	I don't know what is happening... If I try to change thing I will fail	I'm a failure I cannot succeed Its too hard to try to No one udnerstands I am powerless	hyperchondria, confusion, anxiety attacks
ANGER	CONTROL	FEAR OF: ABANDONMENT OR BEING VULNERABLE	I must never let peopl control me. I will control my own destiny. I wont be "weak"	Vulnerable means weak "people like hurting me" I am trapped I am all alone I cant count on people	Rudeness, outbursts, controlling, stubborn easily irritated, sensitive, hold grudges, nit-pick, witholds affection, rages, passive-aggressive,
LUST	RELATION-SHIP	REJECTION SHAME FATHER WOUNDS	I wont open my heart I will keep people at a distance I will reject others before they reject me	I am not needed I am unlovable I am disgusting I don't deserve love	obsessive relationships, porn, masturbatic sex addict sexual identity issues

Christina Marie King

Christina King has been married to Shawn for over 20 years and is the mother of 8 children and they reside in Appleton Wisconsin. She has been speaking for over 16 years Nationally and Internationally on a variety of topics such as Purity, Theology of The Body, Marriage, Pro-life Issues, Family Life, Our Lady of Guadalupe and Healing The Whole Person.

She has appeared on EWTN's "Women of Grace" with Johnette Benkovich, Relevant Radio on numerous occasions and was a speaker with "Catholic Answers" for almost 12 years until they decided to promote in house speakers only.

She is the host of the National Radio Program "Embracing Your Greatness" on Radio Maria. She writes for CatholicMoms.com and has written for Catholic Exchange, Couple to Couple League and her own blogs www.EmbracingYourGreatness.org and EmbracingYourGreatness.blogspot.com

She has an international CD entitled "Pure Freedom" which explains the reason God created us, which is put out by Lighthouse Catholic Media. ParousiaMedia.com carries more of her CD's as well as St. Joseph Communications.

If you like to book Christina to speak at your event please visit CMGBooking.com for details.